ROBOTS HOW INFLUENCE BUSINESS SOCIAL DEVELOPMENT

JOHN LOK

Copyright © John Lok
All Rights Reserved.

Contents

Preface

Introduction

This book concerns to be given my opinions to explain how artificial intelligent technology will impact our life and will influence economic development in the future as well as how to influence human job market change. What kinds of industries which can be applied to replace human job from (AI) learning tools? The most important, I shall indicate what will be (AI) future potential education marketing development in final chapter. I shall give evidences to indicate howand why (AI) will have potential ability to apply to futuer education development from prior all chapters. In labor market part, I shall indicate how artificial intelligence technology influences future macro global economy change. However, I shall explain why (AI) won't replace human teaching job in the final chapter. Although, (AI) will have possible to replace other kind of human occupations, e.g. bus driver, taxi driver, lorry driver, cooker, factory workers etc. different skillful occupations.

Advances in artificial intelligence (AI) technology is for the progress in critical areas, such as health, education, energy, economy inclusion, social welfare and the environment.

Thus, it brings this question: Which (AI) workers be instead of traditional human workers in these different new markets? In recent years, machines had been used to be human's tasks in the performance of certain tasks related to intelligence , such as aspects of image recognition. Experts also forecast that rapid progress in the field of specialized artificial intelligence will continue. Then, it also brings this question: Does (AI) exceed that of human performance on more and more tasks? If it is truth, will some of human jobs to be disappeared? (AI) will be instead of human some simple jobs, then unemployment rate to the low skillful and low educated workers will be increased.

Whether (AI) will be raised either production or performance or unemployment to bring human job market more advantages or more disadvantages? In my this book, I shall explain whether (AI) will bring benefits or disadvantages to human job market. I shall give example to let my readers to think how to support my final view point.

What is future (AI) artificial intelligent products development trend? How to predict consumer behaviors to persuade who to feel (AI) products are more satisfactory to their needs? Why do consumers feel them to need to buy any (AI) products to use? Will it have other similar products to replace (AI) any products?

In this book, I shall give actual data to predict what the future (AI) products development trend is. Giving my opinions to predict how (AI) consumers' choices are more absolutely. I shall concern travel, education, transportation, financial , hospital, administrative service etc. different job natures to indicate how to apply (AI) products to assist these industries more beneficial.

Nowadays, artificial intelligent technology and online technology and online book stores are high technological intelligent product. Hence, human ourselves will have possible to cause artificial intelligent machine men to own human's mind to learn how to read books and/or write books abilities. When artificial intelligent machine men can learn how to read books and/or write books. Consequently, it means that artificial intelligent machine men can own human mind to do any jobs.

In my this book final chapter, I shall assume when artificial intelligent machine men can learn how to write books and/or read books. Then, they will have human's mind ability in possible. Can future artificial intelligent machine men be invented to learn how to write books and/or read books ability? In my this book, I shall attempt to answer this question. Finally, I hope my readers can attempt to make judgement whether artificial intelligent machine men can really learn how to write and/or books. I shall apply online technology to answer this answer. Finally, I shall give my opinions what are the influences when AI machine men had invented to achieve owning human's mind and judgement ability to our future society. The most important, I believe that (AI) technology can be applied to education industry aspect to do teaching or gathering data jobs for teachers. In my next book, I shall explain why and how it can be attempted to apply to education industry.

Prologue

application
- What (AI) function is? p.74-90
- Can (AI) impact human job nature?
- How can human society job nature
to be changed to artificial intelligent society?
- Why does human need artificial intelligence machines?
- How does artificial intelligence influence future working changing in automation employment and productivity aspects?
- Is artificial intelligence possible to replace labor ?
- Can (AI) technology replace human labour nature of work?
- Why can artificial intelligence satisfy human needs?
- Is artificial intelligence one good choice for human future technological benefit?

Chapter Six What is relationship between
(AI) and economy growth
- How can artificial intelligence technology influence economy? p.91-116
- Can (AI) influence global economy growth?
- How can artificial intelligence impact global economy growth?
- What is the relationship between (AI) and (CRM)?
- What is the relationship between
(AI) and global digital economy development ?
    - How can (AI) technology influence digital economy?
- Could work activities in China be automated
making in the nation with the world's largest automation potential?
- Will (AI) technology influence digital economy change to manufacturing industry ?
- What is artificial intelligence potential
benefits and ethical considerations?
- Can (AI) technology impact on customer relationship management (CRM) ?
- How can (AI) technology influence to global
health care economy development?
    Chapter Seven
Artificial intelligence education development
or the future of defense choice
7.1 Online technology and online book
technology influences artificial intelligence

CHAPTER ONE

Competitive influences between artificial intelligence and human job

In my this book, I shall indicate evidences to analyze to answer this topic for my this research aim :

Can robots replace teachers to teach students to learn in schools? Although, (AI) technology will be popular to applied to different jobs, but it still needs social acceptance to replace some human jobs. Today, it is increasingly common for people to use robots in various situations at home and in retail stores, hotels and hospitals. Robots are classified into several types based on their functionality (service and utility robots or those designed to communicate with humans) and appearance (humanoid robots or mechanical robots). The types of robot to which every country attaches particular important in the advance of robotics, reflects the sense of values and preferences of its population . Thus, (AI) will be applied to replace human to do these above different kinds of job nature. For example, U.S. has the highest level of robot utilization at home and an retail stores with its people being the most enthusiastic about the future use of robots. Otherwise, Germany shows a strong tendency to consider robots for industrial purposes, and its people feel strong to the presence of robots in their households. Japanese accepts to apply" human aid robot" that can communicate with humans and they have a high level of familiarity with robots.

Hence, it implied those three countries have accept (AI) to replace human to do any these kinds of job duty and it will influence these three countries' workers lose their old occupations and who will unemployed absolutely, due to many (AI) robots replace them to do their job duties in the future. Also, US will have many retail service workers or retail warehouse workers are unemployed. Germany will have many manufacturing industry's workers are unemployed. Japanese will have many communication industry workers are unemployed, such as telephone service, shopping center services etc. different kind of service industry's service staffs . It will cause these kind of workers' competitive abilities are lost in themselves countries' jobs that require such skills include software developers, court judges, nurses, high school teachers, dentists and university lecturers, these occupations are still difficult to be replaced by (AI) robots.

Are robots taking our jobs or making them? In fact, our societies will have unemployment challenges, even (AI) technology has not created before. However, after (AI) robots invention, some of human jobs will be replaced and it can raise many low skillful and low knowledge level worker unemployment number. However, I think that high productivity driven by increasingly powerful IT -enabled machines is the causes of global labor market problems and accelerating technological change will only make those problems worse, but some occupations which need (AI) to own human's mind, reading, writing, analyzing, speaking abilities. I believe human intelligent robots can not replace human to job, such as teaching jobs. Due to (AI) robots can learn to do simple job, even future (AI) can learn to do difficult job, but some occupations, such as teaching job, (AI) robots can not replace them to do because I believe that (AI) robots can learn how to do teaching or gathering data job duties for educational occupation, but educational researching job duties, (AI) robots won't have ability to attempt to do better to human lectuers.

For exmaple, I suppose that there is a limited amount of labor to be done. The implication is that technology can create unemployment by displacing workers, such as (AI) invention, because the more efficiently worker work (using machines or (AI) robots), the loss work there is for workers to do. Even, any new jobs will be better done by machines or (AI) robots, and unemployment will still skyrocket. How do we know that humans will always be better at some work, or more importantly, enough work, than machines or (AI) robots, e.g. human drivers drive more safe or careful to compare (AI) robot drivers. But, the challenge is that it is not ensure that (AI) robots drivers must not drive careless to cause the chance of accident occurrences more than human drivers. However, technological change can be beneficial to innovation, automation and increasing productivity for businesses. Consequently, although (AI) robots can learn how to drive vehicles to replace drivers, but it is not absolute to ensure (AI) robots can not reduce driving accident occurrence chance to be zero. So, I suppose even, (AI) robot can invent to learn teacher's education knowledge, but it is not represent (AI) robot can attempt to learn human lecturer how to do any educational research job efficiently and effectively and performance perfectly to compare lecturers.

Consequently , it may seem machines can hurt wages and job for low skillful, less educated workers. Also, high educated workers are likely as less educated workers to find themselves displaced and devalued, and more education may create as many problems as it solves. Thus, in negative influence, automation effects on particular jobs shift workers to other jobs that are equally or more desirable. Workers may be highly compensated for possessing human capital that is specialized to a labor market. If technological advance is very rapid, such as (AI) invention, causing a large and very rapid drop in demand in a large labor market, the economy may not be able to absorb the sudden surplus of labor in a short period of timer when (AI) robots are popular to replace some workers to do some occupations in global societies.

For example, self-driving vehicles threaten to send truck drivers to the unemployment office. Computer programs can now write journalistic accounts of sporting events and stock price movement. There are even computers that can grade essay revolutionize some part of teaching jobs. Hence, (AI) robots will have possible to replace human brain to do any judgement, argument, and mind job duties. It implies some occupations which need human' mind will be threaten by (AI) robots, e.g. author, accountant, nurse, engineer. Thus, (AI) robots will have possible to replace some professional and high educated workers' jobs in the future. Although, above these professional occupations have chance to be replaced from (AI) robots because (AI) can spend less time to learn their job abilities easily. But it is not represent (AI) robots can learn teaching occupation workers how to teach students or how to analyze to do educational reseach job easily.

But, technology can create new nature of jobs in possible. For example, a 60 minutes program indicated technology is putting new categories of jobs in the sites (sic) of automation, the 60% of the workforce that makes its living gathering and analyzing information. Also, recession: technology kills middle -class jobs that overall technology is eliminating for more jobs than it is creating by (AI) technology. Hence, human's brain work may be assisted by 60% of (AI) gathering and analyzing information for some occupation , e.g. space scientists, ocean scientists, earth scientists etc. But, it is not represent, (AI) robots can replace these scientists to do their scientifical research job in laboratory. (AI) robots can have ability to learn how to assist scientist to gather and analyze information, but (AI) robots can not learn how to do scientifical research job duties absolutely.

However, I believe the (AI) invention and human job competition may influence global productivity change. Productivity is economic output per unit of input, the unit of on input can be labor hours(labor productivity), but if (AI) robots replace human job, then the unit of input may be (AI) machine hours (AI) robot productivity or all production factors including labors, machines and energy (total factor of productivity). Producing more output with less input can take several forms. Hence, (AI) robots can only replace low skillful and educational level workers, e.g. factory vehicle, clothing, steel etc. products manufacturer workers, public transportation drivers, e.g. bus drivers, tram, train, ferry, taxi, lorry drivers etc. It will bring the benefits to employers reduce these worker numbers, when they are replaced from (AI) robot workers in the future.

The traditional notion of productivity is a form reorganizing production and/or using better or more technology to produce more output per worker hour. But when (AI) robots invention, the form can be reorganizing production and/or using better or more (AI) robots to produce more output per (AI) robot hour. Hence, if the firm apply (AI) robots to produce its products. Then , productivity improvements in the firm may result in less workers employment, due to (AI) robots replace more worker number to achieve more productivity improvement, it has economic benefits (less factor of production) , but more production in long term. Hence, in manufacturing industry, (AI) manufacturing workers can improve productivity, due they can manufacture more product numbers to compare human workers.

Thus, (AI) robots can help any firm to achieve productivity improvement in long term, for example, if unproductve farmers move to the city and start working for high-tech. manufacturers. The shift effect can be more dynamic and disruptive as low-productivity industries lose out in the marketplace to high -productivity industries and the compositional mix of the economy changes. Thus, in the long term (AI) robots can also be beneficial to high productivity industries to bring the mix of economy positive changes.

Moreover, automation will also produce some new jobs in firms that sell the new robot or other labor-saving technology. This means that, in general, there will be shift in the economy in the direction of higher-skill and higher wage jobs. Even if the (AI) robot invention country, US becomes a leader in (AI) robots producing productivity-enhancing technology, it will experience a growth in jobs serving foreign (AI) robots product buyers. Hence, (AI) robots can also create (AI) salespeople, (AI) manufacturing workers , (AI) inventors, scientists, (AI) software designer etc. occupations, when if all society does is move workers from insurance firms, restaurants and car factories to robot factories, productivity will have remained the same to create job needs for insurance, restaurant and car manufacturing worker service occupations for (AI) software designer, (AI) service robots manufacturer, (AI) service robot seller etc. related (AI) service robot product occupation created in (AI) robot technology job market. Hence, (AI) invention also create new (AI) technology job chance. (AI) impacts management job market.

In future, organization management will be changed from (AI) introduction. Division of labor will change and collaboration among humans and machines will increase. Companies will have to adapt their training, performance and talent acquisition strategies to account for a new found emphasis on work that hinges on human
judgement and skills, including experimentation and colloboration.

How (AI) impacts any organizational administrative management work? (AI) 's greatest impact will be on administrative coordination and control tasks, such as scheduling, resource allocation and reporting, (AI)-driven will place a higher premium on what we call " judgement work", the application of human experience and expertise to critical business decisions and practices when information available is insufficient to suggest a successful course of action. This kind of work will require new skills and mindsets; replacing people with machines is not goal in itself. When, artificial intelligence enables cost-cutting automation of routine work, it also empowers value -adding augmentation of human capabilities.

Thus, administrative and routine tasks, such as scheduling, allocation of resources, and reporting, will within intelligent machines, responsibilities that have long been reserved for humans. For instance, a typical store manager or a lead nurse at a nursing home must constantly juggle shift schedules, accounting for staff members' absense owing to illness, vaction, time or sudden departures. Many of these tasks will be automated by (AI).

Imagine (AI) writing management monthly reports, it is not a distant dream. Leading news providers and Wall street banks are now using (AI) report generators to write news and analytical reports by drawing on quantitative data. The associated press, for example, expanded its quarterly earnings reporting from approximately 300 companies to nearly 3,000 with the help of (AI) powered software robots, freeing up journalists to conduct more investigative and interpretive reporting. For another example, Jobalime, a job-placement site, uses intelligent voile analysis algorithms to evaluate job applicants. The algorithm assesses paralinguistic elements of speech, such as tone and inflection, products which emotions a specific voice will elicit, and identifies the type of work at which an applicant will likely excel. In the future , (AI) machines can be applied to assist some kind of office administrative jobs duties. It's attractive to office managers to achieve more accurate judgment to do any administrative matters when who can be assisted from (AI) machines. Thus, managers need to spend time to learn how to apply (AI) machine to assist them to do more accurate judgement, and better informed choices. (AI) robots can be applied to improve the speed quality and cost of available products and services, instead of applying on productivity improvement and administrative improvement aspects. Thus, they may also displace large numbers of workers. This, possibility challenges the traditional benefits model of trying health care and retirement savings to jobs.

In an economy that employs dramatically fewer workers to deliver benefits to displaced workers. For example, the worldwide number of industrial robots has increased rapidly over the past few years. The fall prices of robots, which can operate all day without interruption, make them cost- competitive with human workers. In special consideration, in the service sector, computer algorithums can execute stock trades in a fraction of a second, much faster than any human. As those technologies become cheaper, more capable, and more widespread, they will find even more applicants in an economy.

Consequently, (AI) technology brings unemployed number increasing many businesses continued automating their operations rather than hiring additional workers. A trend among technology companies that receive massive valuations with relatively few workers. For example, in 2014 year Google was valued at $370 billion with only 55,000 employees, a tenth the size of AT & T's workforce in the 1960 year. Hence, if automation technologies like robots and artificial intelligence make jobs less secure in the future, there needs to be a way to deliver benefits outside of employment " flexi security" or flexible security is one idea for providing healthcare, education and housing assistance whether or not someone is formally employed.

In conclusion, (AI) and robots technology will raise unemployment to some occupations when (AI) replaces same industries' workers job duties in our societies in the future, but it also create new jobs to raise employment in any related (AI) robots and automated machine products in (AI) manufacturing. (AI) design, (AI) sale self-related industry, when (AI) replaces same industries' workers' job duties.

CHAPTER TWO

(AI) journalism, media publishing, digital communication technology trend

How to apply (AI) technology in digital communication journalism media, publishing industry? Some scientists indicate future (AI) and digital technology may consist such as: voice driven assistants, emerge. For example, Amazon e book publish applying digital technology and (AI) auto printing technology to sell e books to let readers to listen any e book content by (AI) voice driven speaker when they turn on computer to read e book contents; capable phones start to unlock the possibilities of 3D image of mobile story telling. New smart wearables include ear buds that handle instant translation and glasses that talk and hear. China and India will become a key focus for digital growth with innovations around payment online identity, and artificial intelligence. Thus, future (AI) technology can be applied to 3D image mobile story telling, online payment method to dealt online transaction publishing industry.

Thus, future (AI) technology can be applied to online e book publishing industry to make sound books to let readers feel more attractive . Such as Amazon publish has published sound e books to attract readers to choose to read any its books from online. Also, (AI) technology can also be applied to communication industry. For example, some online pure-play news, opinion and entertainment websites. It is a digital communication media, e.g. online journalism blog (AI) technology can be applied to visual storytellers to let online book readers to enjoy to listen to watch and send any online electronic book contents more attractive. Thus, future (AI) technology will be popular to assist any electronic book publishers to publish visual and sound talking storybook to let readers who can watch motive image and listen and read words from e books more attractive.

Thus, (AI) technology can be applied to internet ecommerce publishing or media industry to help any electronic book publishers to publish sound, image motion electronic book to attract global readers to read, even (AI) technology can be applied to digital entertainment industry, e.g. electronic 3D image virtual video games, computer games. It can be also applied to education industry, e.g. the first true digital native generation and are the native speakers of the digital language of computers to let student to learn different languages or translate words to compare to classroom learning more easily. It can be also applied to communication industry, e.g. (AI) mobile phone. Hence, it seems (AI) technology can be applied to publishing, communication, education , entertainment etc. different industries in the future. (AI) technology will be one kind of tool to satisfy human's daily life needs in the future and these industries has one characteristics is that they need to apply internet to operate to operate to do online business.

Thus, it has three trends of (AI) technology and internet technology need to be linked to achieve one kind of attractive technological business to satisfy client's needs. These three trends as below: All consumer trends involve the internet. It will be many consumer's online habits, shopping, working, socializing, watching TV, studying, travelling, listening. Thus, (AI) music, eating and exercising are just a few examples. This is happening because human usually use mobile broadband or Wi-Fi, rather than cables. Thus, (AI) technology will be applied to mobile to satisfy client's need absolutely.

The mobile phone can be more popular to be used more than computer or laptop tools. The reasons are because women dive the smartphone market by defining mass-market use. But as the speed of technology adoption increases mass market use becomes much quicker then before. Successful new technological products and services , such a (AI) mobile phone products now reach the mass market in popular use. It means that the time period when early adopters influence others is shorter than before. Also, since new products and services increasingly use the internet mass markets are not only faster , but are also more important than ever to consumer themselves. Most internet services become more valuable to individuals when many use them. Thus, it causes why (AI) mobile phone will be popular to be used.

Since, new products and services increasingly use the internet, in the future several trends focus on (AI) smart phone users. Consumers' familiarity with using smartphone apps. Essentially, the technologies will bring other related (AI) and internet service needs, e.g. sound and image emotion e book needs, (AI) mobile communication needs, e-virtual games or e-3D image virtual games etc. entertainment activities needs with such a large part of the world's population now online, it is clear that there is strength in numbers.

Thus, (AI) imagines , if future any (AI) and internet related services or products new technology is easy to use and inexpensive, when the latest products reach the mass market almost as quickly as they reach the early adopters and industry experts. I believe that any (AI) and internet related products or services must be popular to accept to consume for entertainment or useful aim. For example, with major players including Apply, Facebook and Google had invested (AI) technology to develop their businesses. (AI) technology has the potential to disrupt everything in the coming years, from the lives of connected consumers to every industry (AI) will be an alternative route for brands to reach consumers with convincing and relevant messages. Digital technology will assist of the future, then it can improve technology to bring this effect, such as sophisticated software machine learning and speech recognition effective. Hence, Google, Facebook , Yahoo web site service companies can apply (AI) technology to help other companies to advertise their businesses, such as travel, retail, and education etc. industries more attractive. (AI) technology can be applied to internet company to be aware and familiar enough to drive among mainstream consumers, it can create online experience to travel, retail , education and other entertainment needs to online consumers to seek their entertainment needs more easily. Hence, in the future (AI) technology and internet related entertainment service needs will be raised in this (AI) and online consumption market.

 ● (AI) healthcare service industry development

In the future, (AI) medical internet technology tool can be applied to assist individual's health at the center of their focus, e.g. smartwatch compatible mobile app. patients can let personalized reminders for taking their medication snap pictures of their prescriptions to expedite refills, and scan their insurance card. So that, store clerks are prepared with up-to-date patients' information . (AI) owned health operated technological clinics can help patients to receive treatment for minor illnesses, flu shots, cholesterol screenings and more than a dozen other medical services, all of which can be patients who can't make it to a physical location. (AI) healthcare services organizations can provide various telemedicine services. So, patients can receive care via phone or video chat.

For example, one London-based intelligent Brewing company has developed an (AI) system to continuously collect and incorporate customer feedback, which the system itself uses to brew ne various of the company's beers. Thus, the beer clients can give feedback to talk to the algorithm (AI) machine, whenever or anywhere who're drinking the beer. It is such any healthcare services organizations can apply (AI) machine to collect patient's feedback to talk to the algorithum (AI) machine whenever or anywhere who're eating any medicines. So doctors can know every patient's health conditions any time. If the patients feel uncomfortable, the doctor can know from (AI) machine notification to decide whether the patient needs to eat another new medicine or keep to eat same medicine is better. Hence, (AI) medial internet technological body check report machine will be proper to be needed to serve any hospitals' patients in the future.

However , it brings this question. How can (AI) medical internet technological body check report machine apply to hospital more efficient? The essential new medicine co-workers for the health service digital age health service leaders need apply (AI) medical report machines and artificial intelligence to the newest recruits to the workforce bringing new skills to help health service staffs do new jobs and reinventing what's possible, building the health service workforce for today's digital health service demands for patients. Thus, technology-driven health service model innovation from the health service organization outside in and providing digital health service ecosystems for patients to use the (AI) health service equipment will be popular to be accepted to be used.

● I Robot and internet things future machine
men invention

Nowadays, there are some company, which apply internet and (AI) I Robot technology to do any similar human job nature. For fishing industry example, one company, known for creating the Roomba, I Robot is now working with marine conservationists to launch an ocean-patrolling intelligent robot to hunt and manage invasive species, protecting native populations. And evolved industries like precision agriculture are ramping of our increasing population. Area of practice that once seemed impossible to digitize are fundamentally changing because of the impacts of (AI), internet of things capabilities and big data analytics, which have many potentially positive impactions for society.

For textile industry example, automation is nothing new, it has shaped the workplace to replace human jobs to boost productivity in the textile industry. Textile machines have had a generally positive impact over gears, creating value and allowing textile workers to take up more rewarding age will likely continue to create opportunities and lead to new textile industries, companies and textile occupations. It may also compensate for a demographically driven slowdown in the growth of the textile workforce. The future impact of textile (AI) and automatic and internet link is somewhat uncertain. It seems textile industry will be trend to accept (AI) textile workers and internet of thing to replace traditional manual textile workers to produce any shirts, cloths etc. wearing products in factories popularly, during the (AI) textile machine and internet thing technology can be invented to reach the mature stage in the future.

For factory worker transportation job example, they have also expanded their influence, migrating from the factory floor to the service sector and taking the place of humans in a range of activities from financial transactions to transport route optimization. Further (AI) machines and robots are increasingly programmed to learn, meaning they improve with time and undertake cognitive activities. Hence, (AI) machines and internet technology enable automation of work activities to raise factory workers' efficient and performances, also factories can reduce manual worker numbers, due to (AI) machine workers' assistance.

Future, (AI) robotics technologies and internet technique have these different kinds of characteristics: For soft robotics example, it is non-rigid robots construct with soft and deformable materials that can manipulate items of varying size, shape and weight with a single device. For swarm robotics, it coordinated multi-robot systems often involving large numbers of mostly physical robots. For touch/factile robotic example, it robotic body pails (often biologically inspired hands) with capability to sense, touch , dexterity robots example, serpentine robots with many internal degrees of freedom to threat through tightly packed spaces for humanoid robots example, robots physical is similar to human being often bi-pedal that investigate variety capable of performing human tasks , including movement across terrains, object recognition, speech sensing etc. For autonomous cars and trucks example, it is capable of operating with a human pilot, e.g. the unarmed general atomics Predator XPUAV with roughly half the wingspan of a Boeing 737 can fly autonomously for up to 35 hours from take-off to landing, for unmanned aerial vehicles example, flying vehicles capable of operating without a human pilot, the unarmed general atomics predator -XPUAV , with roughly half the wingspan of a Boing 737, and fly autonomously for up to 35 hours from take off to landing, for (AI) chat bots example, (AI) systems designed to simulate conversation with human users, particularly those integrated into massaging apps.

In Dec. 2015. the general service administration of the US Govt. described how it used a chat bot named Mrs. Landingham (a character from the television show the west wing) to help onboard new employees. Finally, for robotic process automation example, class of software robots that replicates the actions of a human being interacting with the user interfaces of both software systems. Enables the automation of many back-office work flows without requiring expensive IT integration . Hence, future (AI) robot machine men will have different functions to be applied to different industries to use in possible.

Statistics Denmark shows that (AI) automation potential robots will influence few jobs are completely automatable , but close to half consists of 40% automatable tasks: It showed example occupations include share of automated, such as brewing machine operators are more than 80%, logging equipment operators are more than 50%, roofers , stock tasks clerks, travel agent are more than 50%, farmers , nursing assistants are more than 30%, physicians, teachers , managers are more than 10%.

For example, humans perform a wide variety of tasks from planting corn to examine spreadsheets, meeting clients and lifting crates in a store. Each of these actions requires a combination of innate or acquired capabilities, internet technique assistance, ranging from social perceptiveness to fine motor skills and natural language understanding. To understand and map automation feasibility by existing technology. Mc Kinsey has developed a framework of 18 technical capabilities that can substitute tasks performed by humans. The capabilities are grouped in five categories: sensory, cognitive, language, social and emotional and physical. So, it seems (AI) robot machine men and internet technique will have possible combination to invent to own human's emotion , language, learning, task skill abilities.

Mckinsey global institute analysis also showed current technologies have achieved different levels of human performance across 18 capabilities include: sensory perception, autonomously infer and integrate complex input using sensors, cognitive capabilities reorganizing known patterns/ categories supervised learnings, generating novel, logical reasoning/ problem solving, optimization and planning, creative, information retrieval, coordination with multiple agents, output articulation/presentation, national language processing, social and emotional capabilities-natural language understanding, social and emotion sense, reasoning output, physical capabilities-fine motor skills, navigation mobility. Hence, it seems (AI) robots and internet technological will combine to invent to own human' some skills to replace human to do some kind of tasks in possible.

In conclusion, future (AI) robot and internet will be needed to link to cooperate together to raise human's work efficiency in popular.

CHAPTER THREE

How artificial intelligence replaces human job possibility

What is the risk of automation for jobs to replace human job? In recent years, there has been a revival of concerns that automation and digitalization night after all result in jobless future. As I argue, this might lead to an overestimation of job (AI) automate , as occupations labelled as high-risk occupations often still contain a substantial share of tasks that are hard to automate.

For example, when the share of (AI) automatable jobs is 6% in Korea, the corresponding share is 12% in Australia. Differences between countries may reflect general differences in workplace organization, differences in previous investments into (AI) automation technologies as well as differences in the education of workers across countries. I also discover that (AI) automation and digitalization are unlikely to destroy large numbers of jobs. But, however, low qualified labors are likely to raise costs as the (AI) automate of their jobs is higher compared to highly qualified workers.

In fact, (AI) technology will influence some new technology to replace some human's job, such as driverless car, the largely autonomous smart factory , service robots or 3D printing. These technologies are driven by advances in computing power, robotics and artificial intelligence and ultimately redefine what type of human capabilities machines are able to do.

Hence, question brings whether (AI) invention will influence general human jobs to be replaced by (AI) autonomous jobs? Whether will the potential foe automation with actual employment loss? In particular, the technical possibility to use (AI) machines rather tasks need not mean that the substitution of humans by machines actually takes place.

Whether (AI) technology replaces human's some job, it is beneficial to our society or not. Instead, machines are increasingly capable of performing non-routine cognitive tasks, such as driving or legal writing . In particular, advances in the field of machine learning (ML), e.g. computational statistics and visions, data mining, artificial intelligences allow for automating cognitive task, when the use of (ML) in mobile robotics (MR) also allows for automating certain manual tasks. So, it seems, (AI) technology can replace some labor job, e.g. warehouse transportation, even mind's job, e.g. legal writing, driving in possible.

For example, if (AI) automatic non-manual driving can reduce hurt or death risk, it is beneficial to our society, or (AI) automatic robots can more any heavy things (products) in warehouse safely. Then, it can reduce the warehouse labor's bodies hour risk, it is beneficial to the workers. Even, if (AI) robot can write any legal documents, no any word errors in short time. It is beneficial to the law companies , but it also bring unemployment chance, due to these jobs can be replaced by (AI) robots to do in the future. Hence, it will cause some occupation to be disappeared, due to (AI) robots can do our these kinds of jobs in the future.

Frey & Osborne (2013) reported these kinds of occupations will be replaced by (AI) robots in possible. They include computer, engineering, financial, management, legal , art and medium, community service, education, healthcare practitioners and technical service, sales and related, office and administrative support, farming, fishing and forestry, construction and extraction, installation, maintenance, and repair , production, transportation and material moving. It seems our future some professional occupations will have possible to the replaced by (AI) robots to replace, instead of labor jobs. Hence, (AI) robots technology will have much trend to replace high knowledge or low knowledge skillful labors in the future.

In conclusion, it implies that only using information on task-usage at the individual level leads to significantly lower estimates of jobs " at risk", some workers in occupations with according to high automate nevertheless often perform tasks with are hard to automate. Why can (AI) replace human to do some kinds of jobs? (AI) artificial intelligence refers to the ability of a computer or a computer enable robotic system to process information and produce outcomes in a manner similar to the thought process of humans in learning, decision making and solving problem. By extension, the goal of (AI) systems is to develop systems to capable of tasking complex problems in ways similar to human's logic and reasons who feel in our future. Hence, it means future (AI) robots has effort to replace human to do any jobs in possible.

3.1 (AI) directions for future non-manual control road vehicles market

Future road vehicle products and technologies must meet social, economic and environmental protection and driving safety goals , and satisfying market requirements for mobility, accident reducing, performance, cost desirability. Thus, (AI) auto-non manual control vehicles need to be followed this direction to invent. To satisfy future driver's safety of needs, enhanced vehicle speed desired functional performance of road transportation system, required and desired technological response, including research needs. It is long term up to 20 years vision, for (AI) auto non-manual research. Thus, (AI) auto non manual vehicle manufacturers need often to revise their (AI) vehicles functions to raise to improve their system performance and driving industry driver's needs, e.g. private drivers need or public transportation driver's need or business client's need. Hence, future (AI) transportation will need have individual driving consumer and business driving consumer both targets.

Thus, future (AI) automation manual control vehicles need to deliver high impact technology solutions to meet social , economic and environmental and safe goals. Engine needs to be improved efficiency , performance, drivability, reliability, durability and speed-to-market together with reduced emissions and cost; hybrid, electric and alternatively fuel (AI) non manual control vehicle technology development, leading to new fuel and power systems, such as hydrogen, fuel cells and batteries, which satisfy future social, economic and environmental and safe goals. Software, sensors, electronics and telematics technology development are needed to be lead to improve vehicle performance, control and adaptability, intelligent , mobility and security, structure and materials technology development, leading to improved safety, performance and leading to flexibility with reduced cost and environmental pollution to achieve the (AI) non manual drivers to feel (AI) vehicle performance, auto control and adaptability is better to compare traditional manual driving vehicles.

In fact, in traditional manual driving market, Japan and USA had had over 80% of world car production by six major global groups. In the future, it is possible only USA can dominate (AI) non manual auto driving vehicle manufacturing market if Japan had no effort to manufacture any (AI) auto non manual control vehicles. So, it means that it is only Japan is USA potential (AI) auto non manual control vehicle manufacturing competitors. Also, it means that it is only USA has effort to export (AI) auto non manual control vehicles to global (AI) auto non manual control vehicle market.

Thus, in long term, (AI) non manual control vehicle product market development, USA (AI) vehicle manufacturers will have these requirement to win new technological competition to traditional manual control vehicle. The requirements include: low cost fuel, low carbon, fuel cell and telematics technologies, the technological roadmap function, such as detailed consideration clear provision of other important areas to the drivers. When the (AI) non manual auto drivers are sitting in the non manual control auto vehicle. Although, who does not need to drive, but who need to know how to go to anywhere by electric road map show clearly. So, the driver won't lose direction and he/she can know the (AI) non manual control vehicles is driving to anywhere in any time, even when who is sleeping.

In the future, the (AI) non manual control vehicles need to be invented to satisfy any business , transportation clients' needs, instead of individual clients needs, e.g. cans, trucks, buses, emergency and utility vehicles, trains, trams etc. Hence, technological road mapping is one important tool to help any business, transportation (AI) non manual control vehicle clients. Technological roadmap is a technique that is used in industry to support strategic planning for (AI) non manual driving vehicles in the future. Electronic road maps generally take the form of multi-layered time based charts, linking technology developments to future (AI) non manual control vehicle market requirements.

Technology road mapping is a flexible technique and the roadmap architecture and process for developing the roadmap most generally be customized to meeting the particular aims. Why technology roadmap will be popular to (AI_ non manual control vehicles. It's advantages include: It is a technology solutions and options that can enable the performance targets to be achieved engine hybrid, electric and alternatively fueled vehicles, software, sensors electronics and telematics, structures and materials design and manufacturing process. It is road transport system performance measures and targets tool, in response to the trends and get (AI) non manual control vehicle drivers to get society, economy, environment protection, low cost driving benefits, also it can help any transportation clients to know how to go to anywhere clearly. Hence, technological road map will be one good tool to assist (AI) non manual control auto vehicle to develop future road driving market.

Reference(source)

Frey & Osborne (2013), The future of employment: How susceptible are jobs to computerization? University of Oxford.

Mckinsey Global Institute Analysis

Statistics Denmark, Global automation impact model, Makinsey analysis

CHAPTER FOUR

(AI) -driven automation industry development

(AI) -driven automation industry will create wealth and expand economy growth to any countries, but it will be accompanied by changed in the skills that workers need to learn. One of main ways that technology increases productivity is by decreasing the number of labor hours needed to create a unit of output. It implies (AI) technology will influence low educated and low skillful labor number to be decreased (reduction employment number).

In contrast, technological change tended to work in a different direction throughout the nowadays. The advance of computer and the internet raised the relative productivity of higher skilled workers. So, routine-intensive occupations that focused on predictable tasks disappearance, such as switch board, operators, filming checkers, travel agents and assembling line workers etc. were particularly replaced by new technologies.

However, today, it may be challenging to predict exactly which jobs will be most immediately affected by (AI) driven-automation. The reason is because (AI) is not a single technology, but rather a collection of technologies that are felt unevenly through the economy to influence job changing both negatively and positively. In positively view point, (AI) driven-automation will make many workers more productive and increase demand for certain skills. Consequently, new jobs are likely to be directly create in areas , such as the development and supervision of (AI) as well as indirectly created in a range of areas throughout the economy as higher incomes lead to expanded demand. Otherwise, in negatively view point, many traditional human needed (demand) skillful jobs will be threatened by automation are highly concentrated among lower-paid, lower-skilled and less -educated workers. It means automation will cause pressure on demand for this group, pressure and employment, if (AI) can replace the low skilled and less educated workers' jobs. Thus, (AI) will have negative influence to impact on the labor market.

(AI) capabilities will enable automation of some tasks that have long required human labor. Why can (AI) replace some simple human jobs? For example, advances in robotics are expanding machines' abilities to interact with and sharp the physical world. Combined , (AI) and robotics will give rise to smarter machines that can perform more sophisticated functions than ever before and brings more advantages that humans have exercised. This will permit automation of many tasks now performed by human workers and could change the shape of the labor market and human activity.

4.1 How (AI) influences labor market

Today, it may be challenging to predict exactly which jobs will be most immediately affected by (AI)-driven automation. Because (AI) is not a single technology, but rather a collection of technologies that are applied to specific tasks.

Some specific predictions are possible based on the current (AI) technology. For example, driving jobs and house cleaning jobs, bank counter service jobs, telephone enquiry service operators. Restaurant cooking jobs, simple accounting record service jobs etc. that require relatively less education to perform. Advancements in computer vision and related technologies have made the feasibility of fully appear more likely, potentially displacing some workers in driving-dominant professions. Seemingly similar robot, for which the operational tasks is less specific of navigating to a specific destination when following a set of given rules and preserving safety.

In the future, the effects of (AI) on the labor market in the decade ahead will continue the trend toward skill-biased change that computerization and communication innovations have driven in recent decades. Thus, some human driving occupation will be disappeared or replaced by (AI) automation driven. For example, bus drivers, light truck or delivery services drivers, heavy and tractor-trailer truck drivers, school drivers, tax drivers, travel bus drivers.

However, (AI) technology could enable some workers to focus time on other job responsibilities, boosting their productivity, and actually raised wage growth among those still holding the reshaped jobs. For example, salespeople, who currently spend a considerable amount of time driving could find themselves able to do other work when a car drives them from place to place, or inspectors and appraisers could fill out paperwork, when their car drives itself. This (AI) -driven technology should make these workers more productive, with (AI) -driven technology serving as a complement, not a substitute. New jobs will also likely be created, both in existing occupations cheaper transportation costs with lower prices and increase demand for products and all the related occupations, such as service and fulfillment, and in new occupations not currently foreseeable.

What kind of jobs will be created by (AI) technology? Predicting future job growth is extremely difficult, due to it depends on technologies or substitute for existing today as well as they may complement or substitute for existing human skills and jobs. However, (AI) will also lead to substantial indirect job creation to the degree it raises productivity and wages, it may also lead to higher consumption that would support additional jobs from high-end draft production to restaurant and retail. The future(AI) " augmented intelligence", the technology's role is as assisting and expanding the productivity of individuals rather than replacing human work. Thus, based on the biased-technical change framework, demand for labor will likely increase the most in the areas where humans complement (AI) automation technologies. For example, (AI) technology , such as IBM's Watson may improve early detection of some cancers or other illnesses, but a human healthcare professional is needed to work with patients to understand and translate patients' symptoms, inform patients of treatment options, and guide patients through treatment plans. Shipping companies may also partner workers who pick up and deliver products over the last feet with (AI) enabled autonomous vehicles that move workers efficiently from site to site. In such cases, (AI) augments what a human is able to do and allows individuals to either be move effective in their specially task or to operate on a larger scale. Thus, it seems (AI) technology will also create new jobs, raise productivities and workers' efficiencies.

4.2 Redefining management in
the workforce of artificial intelligence
In the future, due to artificial intelligence influences to some kind of human jobs nature. So, the kind of human jobs of management methods will also need to change to adapt the artificial intelligence technology input to their organizations. It will cause challenges for every executive and manager if who won't have effort to manage their teams how to apply artificial

intelligence technology to work efficiently and easily. For example, division of labor will change among humans and machines will increase. Thus, companies will have to adapt their training performance and talent strategies how to emphasize on work that how to make human judgment and skills and experimentation. Thus, (IA)'s greatest impact will be on administrative coordination and control tasks, such as scheduling , resource allocation.

In fact, mangers will encounter this challenges: How to apply human experience and expertise to judge critical business decisions and practices when the information available is insufficient to suggest a successful course of action? Due to this kind of work will require new skills and mindsets. I shall indicate these change management methods to adapt (AI) technology. Such as: administration and routine tasks, scheduling , allocation of resources and reporting will fall within the intelligence machines, responsibilities that have long been reserved for humans. For example, a typical store manager or a lead nurse at a nursing home most constantly arrange shift schedules, accounting for staff members' absences owing to illness, vacation time or sudden departures.

Thus, the managers need to learn how to arrange new division of labor within the organizations after (AI) technology had been implemented to the organization. Artificial intelligence is currently influencing into once considered exclusive to humans: assessing and acting on human emotions and personality traits. The influences to managers need to change their strategies to adapt (AI) technology implements include such as below:

Firstly, managers need to spend the bulk of their time on coordination and control tasks from intelligent system implements. Their time spending on these major three aspects from impact of intelligent system: coordinate and control, solve problems and collaborate and people and community , strategy and innovation three aspects. Thus (AI) will influence managers need to change their judgment method to teach whose teams how to adapt the (AI) system operations in any organizations.

Secondly, (AI) will influence top, middle and low level management needs to change to adapt the (AI) technology operations to any owned (AI) technology organizations in the future. Intelligent machines must be trained in context. Just like humans , on-the-job training is a requirement for such machines because they typically arrive with only very general capabilities. To get the most from (AI), managers at all levels must participate in the instructional experience and in the learning process and provides managers' familiarity with such systems on these aspects, e.g. How the system works and generate advice, how the system has a proven track record , how the system provides convincing explanations , how the system can make simple rule- based decisions.

Thirdly, managers need to learn how to make judgment more accurate (AI) systems assistance. Although (AI) will invariably take on more routine work and even augment human decision-making, it won't judgment work, the application of human experience and expertise to critical business decisions when the information available is insufficient to suggest a successful course of action or reliable enough to suggest an obvious course of action. For a sense of the nature of judgment work, consider big data marketing and sales analytics. Such analytics often provide insights that can inform promotional campaigns, including predicting which promotions will generate desired sales brand further into the future, marketing executives need use judgment, combining analytics with their own and others' insight and experience.

The application of experience and expertise to critical business decisions and practice represents the real value of human judgment. But, when artificial intelligent machines are implemented to any organizations to assist the low, middle and top level management to make any business judgment. These forms of judgment work that managers can gather data interpretation, idea development more absolute from (AI) machine assistance. Thus, why these level management executives need to learn how to apply (AI) machines to help them to make any business judgment more accurate.

4.3 How (AI) influences organizational change

Consequently creative and social intelligence will be in even greater demand as (AI) makes in management and the workforce. This development will represent a long term trend in labor markets , one characterized by intensifying demand and reward for social skills with a growing desire for creative capabilities, managers will seek to fashion of ideas and hypotheses from inside and outside of the enterprise to shape solutions to their most pressing business problems. Thus, (AI) will influence overall organizational team members who have chance to participate any decision to make more accurate business judgment.

Many managers mistakenly view judgment work as only an individual discipline, failing to appreciate that it can also involve decide interpersonal and organizational practices. In more complex settings, judgment is typically a collective outcome of individuals' and teams' diverse perspectives, insights and experiences. And often , the resulting choices are better informed than decisions that an individual would have arrived at on his or her own.

Thus, when any organizations apply (AI) technology to assist managers to gather data and ideas to make any judgment. In these cases, organizations can create the conditions for effective collective judgment by establishing structures , such as " shadow advisory boards" that prompt managers and employees to source and synthesize multiple perspectives. Thus, a traditional organization (firm) might freshen its thinking is t put together a shadow advisory board, comprised of young, digital people who can apply (AI) machine assistance to make judgment work more accurate whether related to people development, problem-solving or strategizing and innovating for considerable degrees of creative and social intelligence.

Thus, on the one hand, (AI) technology machine augmentation and automation can give these advantages to human (organization managers) , e.g. developing people and community, solving problems and collaborating, coordinating and controlling work, shaping strategy and leading innovation. Besides, on the other hand, the next generation managers need have these individual attitude to treat intelligent machines to be as colleagues.

When, judgment is a human skill, intelligent machines can accelerate human learning that supports it, assisting in data -driven simulations, scenarios and search and discovery activities. Focuses on judgment work, some decisions require insight beyond what data can tell them. This is the sweet sport for human judgment, the application of experience and expertise to critical business decisions and practices. Thus, managers will also need to find ways to learn how to use digital (AI) technologies to tap into the knowledge and judgment of partners, customer external stakeholders and role models in other industries after the (AI) machine had been implemented to the organization.

4.4 Future works change:
Automation, employment
and productivity

Human future " micro to macro" industry trends will be affected business strategy and public policy by (AI) technology. In the future (AI) technology will influence those six themes: productivity and growth, natural resources, labor markets, the evolution of global financial markets, the economic impact of technology and innovation and urbanization.

However, (AI) technology will bring economic benefits of tackling gender inequality, a new global competition, Chinese innovation and digital globalization.

Nowadays, advances in robotics artificial intelligence, and machine learning are in a new age of automation, as machines match or outperform human performance in a development to any countries. For example, automation of activities can enable businesses to improve performance by reducing errors and improving quality and speed, and in some cases achieving outcomes that go beyond human capabilities. For example, some research indicated automation could raise productivity growth globally by 0.8 to 1.4 % annually; more than 2,000 work activities across 800 occupations. When less than 5% of all occupations can be automated using demonstrated technologies about 60% of all occupations have at least 30% of constituent activities that could be automated. Many occupations will change that will be automated away: Activities most susceptible to automation involve physical activities, in highly structured and predictable environments, as well as the collection and processing of data. They are most prevalent in manufacturing , accommodation and food service and retail trade and include some middle-skill jobs. For example, such as natural language processing is a key factor. Beyond technical feasibility, the cost of technology competition with labor including skills and supply and demand dynamics, performance benefits including and beyond labor cost savings, and social and regulatory acceptance will be affected by (AI) automation technology. Thus, (AI) automation will impact to influence global employment in those aspects as below:

Firstly, assuming that people are displaced by automation will find other employment. The anticipated shift in the activities in the labor force is of a similar order as the long-term shift away from agriculture and decreases in manufacturing share of employment. Both of manufacturing and agriculture industries which would be accompanied by the creation of new types of work not foreseen at the time.

Secondly, for business, the performance benefits of automation are relatively clear. Thus, the businessmen have opportunities for their micro economies to benefits from the productivity growth potential and macro economies to benefit to encourage continued progress and innovation , investment and market incentives. At the same time, employers must innovate policies to help workers and institutions adapt to the impact on employment.

This will likely include rethinking education and training, income support and safety nets , as well as support for those dislocated, when employees need to leave themselves homes to move to other cities to learn new (AI) automation works. Thus, individuals in the workplace will need to engage move comprehensively with machines as part of their everyday activities, and acquire new skills that will be in demand in the new automation age. Consequently , the scale of shifts in the labor force over many decades that automation technologies can be a similar order to the long -term technology -enables shifts in the developed countries' workforces away from agriculture in the 21 th century. Those shifts did not result in long-term mass unemployment because they were accompanied by the creation of new types of work not foreseen at the time. However, human will still be needed in the workforce when the total productivity gains are caused by (AI) technology.

4.5 What occupations will be influenced by (AI) technology.

In the future, scientists predict that these occupations will be influenced by (AI) technology mostly. They include : retail salespeople, food and beverage service workers, language or translation teachers, health practitioners. Since these work activities have a more relevant occupations are made up of a range of activities with different potential for (AI) automation . For example, a retail salesperson will spend more time interacting with customers, stocking shelves , or ringing up sales. Each of these activities is distinct and requires different capabilities to perform successfully.

Thus, these job activities have similar simple control characteristics. Simple activities include greet customers, answer questions about products and services, clean and maintain work areas, demonstrate product feature process sales and transactions. All these activities can have similar simple activities in order to (AI) machines can be learn how to do these activities from (AI) technology . For example, the capability perception includes sensory perception, cognitive capabilities, such as retrieving automation, recognizing known patterns(supervised learning), logical reasoning problem solving.

Thus, (AI) machine is such human, which has feeling and emotion, such as social and emotional sensing, judgement reasoning methods, natural language understanding and physical capabilities, such as mobility , navigation, gross motor skill, fine motor skills. It seems that the future,

(AI) human invents machines which will have these human characteristics to do human similar behavioral job duties more easily and efficiently. It implies these above human occupations will be replaced by (AI) human invention machines in the future. Due to (AI) creation, it is possible to cause unemployment number of these above workers will increase because (AI) machines can do their similar job behavioral activities.

Consequently, employers won't need to employ many of these skillful labor. Otherwise, they can buy less number (AI) machines to attempt to do whose job activities more easily and efficiently. So, it seems (AI) machines will have more high work performance to replace these occupation workers' work performance. Finally, these occupation worker unemployment number will only increase when the (AI) machines had been invented to achieve to do their work behavioral activities absolutely success in the future.

4.6 Whether (A) technology machine labor
will replace human worker more or assist
human worker more

There is no single agreed definition of a robot how outcome of a task that is completed without human intervention. When some definitions require the task to be completed by a physical machine moves and respond to its environment, other definitions use the term robot in connection with tasks completed by software , without physical embodiment.

However, to answer the question : Whether (AI) technology machine labor will replace human worker more or assist human worker more. I shall indicate some examples to let readers to judge whether (AI) technology can create new jobs or reduce old jobs.

Firstly, I shall explain what (AI) function is. (AI) is a service robot that performs useful tasks for humans or equipment excluding industrial automation application . Thus, the classification of a robot into industrial robot or service robot is done according to its intended application. It is also a personal service robot or a service robot for personal used for a non commercial task, usually by lay persons . Examples are domestic servant robot, and pet exercising robot. It is also a professional service robot or a service robot for professional used for a commercial task, usually operated by a properly trained operator. Examples, are cleaning robot for public places, delivery robot in offices or hospitals, fire-fighting robot, rehabilitation robot and surgery robot in hospitals. Thus, these functions will be future (AI) application to our daily life necessaries or business necessaries.

However, some authors agree (AI) will bring negative outcomes of automation, due to raise competiveness, reduce human job nature. Otherwise, other authors argue (AI) will bring positive outcomes of automation, due to raise productivities, job creation, assist humans work.

On the positive outcome hand, robots can increase productivity . This is particularly important for small-to medium sized businesses both are in developed and developing countries economies. It also enables large companies to increase their competitiveness through faster product development and delivery. Increased use of robot is also enabling companies in high cost countries to re shore, or bring back to their domestic base parts of the supply chain that will have previously outsourced to sources of cheaper labor. Currently , the greater threat to employment is not a automation, but an inability to remain competitive. Automation has led overall to an increase in labor demand and positive impact on wages. The reason is that the middle-income/middle-skilled jobs have reduced as a proportion of overall contribution to employment and earnings leading to fears of increasing income inequality, the skills range within the middle income bracket is large. Thus, robots are driving an increase in demand for workers at the higher -skilled and with a positive impact on wages. This issue is how to enable middle-income earners in the lower-income range to unskilled or retain. Finally, the (AI) positive impact supporter who argue the future will be robots and humans can work together.

However, on the negative outcome hand, robots can substitute labor activities, but don't replace jobs. They believe that less than 10% of jobs are fully automatable. Increasingly , robots are used to complement and augment labor activities, the net impact on jobs and the quality of work is positive. Automation can provide the opportunity for humans to focus on higher-skilled, higher-quality and higher-paid tasks. Robots can improve productivity when they are applied to tasks that which perform more efficiently and to a higher and more consistent level of quality than humans. For example, increased productivity is enabling some firms, such as Whirlpool, Caterpillar and Ford Motors company in the US restructure their supply chains, bringing back parts of the manufacturing process to the country of origin. Thus, productivity gains due to robotics and automation are important not just at the company level, but also for build industry and nation competitiveness.

I suppose that productivity can be raised. What are the impacts of robots on employment? Firstly, the main focus of development has been on personal entertainment, which does not drive worker productivity (manufacturing production). When the internet (information and communication technology (ICT)) innovation. This is borne and by findings that manufacturing productivity, which has been driven by innovations in automation rather than consumer technologies, has government strongly than productivity in the services sectors of the economy in most nature economies. It seems (AI) automation will create many jobs in internet communication entertainment game industry. For example, many young people like to use internet to play any electronic games from computer or mobile at home or outside home conveniently. Thus, (AI) automation will increase demand to be invented to any new entertainment game from internet channel. It will need to employ many (AI) entertainment game inventors to create many automation entertainment games. Thus, (AI) automation in internet entertainment game industry will need human (AI) entertainment game inventors to invent the knowledge-based capital of (AI) automation entertainment games. The (AI) entertainment game inventors will need own research and development skills, form specific skills, organizational know-how skills, databased knowledge, design and various forms of intellectual property to do these (AI) automation entertainment game invention occupations in the future.

International Federation Of Robotics(2016) indicated that China will be as a major robotics manufacturer and user of robots, benefiting from jobs created by robot manufacturing and productivity gains from robot use. Chins had sold of robots to any one single market every year since 2017 year. The Chinese government has included a focus on robotics in its 10 year strategy. In order to achieve its target of a robot density of 150 units per 10, 000 workers by 2020 year. Thus, Chinese companies will have to install around 650,000 new industrial robots between 2016 to 2020 year, 2.5 times more than installed globally in 2015 year.

Hence, China (AI) manufacturing industry will need to employ many workers . It implies (AI) manufacturing industry will create many new occupations in China. Also, ministry of economy, trade and industry (2015) also showed that Japan currently has the largest stock of industrial robots in operations, primarily in the automation industry. Driven by a rapidly aging population and low productivity rates, the Japanese government has sights on a 20-fold increase in the use of robots in the non-manufacturing sector and a three-fold growth rate of labor productivity in the service sector both by 2020 year. Thus, it also implies Japan will need many robots to be provide to service industry. Due to robots will provide to serve any businessmen's clients. Thus, it is possible that the service workers won't be dismissed as well as it is depended on the serving job nature to decide whether Japan's service workers can still serve to their employer when the service (AI) robots are applied to whose employers.

Consequently, it seems that (AI) can create employment, Ministry of economy, trade and industry (2015) showed that such as China will develop the major (AI) automation manufacturing industry. The (AI) employers will need to employ many workers to manufacture any these different kinds of (AI) robots to satisfy China or overseas individual or business buyers needs. But, (AI) can also cause unemployment to the low skillful service workers. Such as if Japan some service businesses choose to buy any (AI) service robots to replace their service staffs to serve their clients. It is possible that the service staffs will be dismissed, due to (AI) robots can do such as their same service job duties to achieve better service performance. Thus, today, it is increasingly common for people to use robots in various situations at home and in retail stores, hotels and hospitals these service industries. Robots are classified into server types based on their functionality (service and utility robots or those designed to communicate with humans) and appearance (humanoid robots or mechanical robots). The type of robot, to which each country allocated particular importance in the advance of robotics, reflects the sense of values and preferences of its population. Thus, if the country has high population needs to use robots, then they will influence either more new jobs creation or more old job loss in the country's (AI) manufacturing or (AI) service industries both. For example, Japan respondents often associate the term " robot " with humanoid robots that can communicate with human and they have a high level of familiarity with robot. The US has the highest level of robot utilization at home and in retail stores with its people being the most enthusiastic about the future use of robots. Germany shows a strong tendency to consider robots for industrial purposes and its people feel strong effort to the presence of robots in their households.

In conclusion, to judge whether how (AI) will influence the country's employment to be better or worse. It will depend on the country home buyers (users) or business buyers (users) how to use (AI) for their daily needs. If the country , such as US retail stores need to use (AI) , it will have possible to reduce some or many retail service workers. Even, if the country , such as Japan has many home users need to use (AI) , it will not influence the employment market. Otherwise, it will raise (AI) salespeople numbers. Even, if the country, such as Germany and China will have many (AI) manufacturers, then it will create many (AI) manufacturing occupations for these (AI) manufactory workers.

Consequently, (AI) robots manufacturing and service needs will have positive or negative impact to any country's employment. It will depend on the (AI) service provision and service workers' job nature as well as the manufacturing workers of (AI) knowledge level to decide their employment chance in their country's employment market.

CHAPTER FIVE

Artificial intelligence(AI) learning tools application

● What (AI) function is?

Some scientists explain that artificial intelligence means which is an expert system, computer software that embodies a portion of the specialized knowledge of a human portion in a specific, narrow domain, owns decision making ability of human expert. The (AI)technology is based on the premise that what makes a person an expert is years of experience that enables who recognizes certain patterns in a problem as being similar to pattern. For example, in the future artificial intelligence system can be applied to control air traffic, design to computer configuration, medical diagnosis, instruction/training, speech/interpretation, monitoring to (nuclear plant), planning to mission, factory scheduling, prediction weather, repairing telephone, automatic driving etc. different industries.

Artificial intelligence characteristics include: creative, adaptive , common sense, fact processing, quick replication, broad focus permanent and consistent skill. Otherwise, traditional computer expert system disadvantage includes perishable, unpredictable, slow reproduction, expensive, slow reproduction, slow processing lacks inspiration, needs instruction, narrow focus only machine knowledge. So, artificial intelligence is a branch of computer science devoted to creating computer to influence software and hardware to attempt to create human intelligence or human intelligent behavior. It is learning from experience, responds flexibility in situation that are, new or not anticipated.

Thus, (AI) can be learnt programmed knowledge to solve problems, using reasoning in solving problem, understanding and inferring facts and rules, recognizing the relative importance of different elements in a situation. In summary, artificial intelligence is concerned with two basic ideas mainly:

The first idea, it involves studying the thought processes of humans to understand what intelligence is; the second idea, it deals with representing thought processes using companies to create artificially intelligent entities for testing the theories of intelligence.

● Can (AI) impact human job nature?

Human need concern this question: Will artificial intelligence (AI) reduce some human jobs in order to instead of replacing machines to do? Due to artificial intelligence is the ability of machines to do thing, that people would require intelligence. For example, artificial intelligence machine man driving(self-driver), it (AI) machine man driving research is an attempt to discover and describe aspects of human intelligence that can be simulated by driving machine functions. Alternatively, (AI) mathematical research may be another viewed as an attempt to develop a mathematical theory function to describe the abilities and actions of things (natural or man-made) exhibiting intelligent behavior and server as a design of intelligent calculation machine function.

Why do humans need artificial intelligence machines to instead of traditional human service job? For example, can artificial intelligence machine man (self-driving) driver drive to replace human driver? I shall compare the differences between humans and computers : The characteristics of humans are good at recognizing various things, either seen before or not, recognizing the relationship patterns between things. Human thinking is common sense reasoning, combining all types of sensory input, acting appropriately in novel situations, learning new things and changing behavior patterns, making decisions , even when given incomplete information, working with noisy, incomplete information gathering behaviors . However, characteristics of computers are good at: The tasks humans do naturally are extremely difficult for a computer program as intelligent, which must be able to do the same kind of tack as humans do naturally.

Hence, (AI) is an combination of many different success and technologies: Linguistics - computational and socio, philosophy-logic, philosophy of mind and of language, electronical engineering -image and speech processing, pattern recognition, robotics, machine learning, neural networks, optimization scheduling, management information system and decision making. So, it is possible that (AI) can impact human job nature to instead of human working behavior in the future.

● How can human society job nature
to be changed to artificial intelligent society?

From the first intelligent perspective reason view point, artificial intelligence is making machines " intelligent" acting as humans expect people to act. Artificial intelligence has ability to distinguish computer responses from human responses, it owns knowledge to solve expert problem. From another research perspective reason view point, artificial intelligence is the study of how to make computers do things which, at the moment, people do better (Rich & Knight, 1991, p.3).

(AI) researchers are native in a variety of domains, e.g. formal tasks (mathematics, games), tasks (perception, robotics, natural language, common sense reasoning), expert tasks (financial analysis, medical diagnostics, engineering, scientific analysis and other areas).

From the second business perspective reason view point, (AI) is a set of many powerful tools, and methodologies for using those tools to solve business problems. From a programming perspective reason view point, (AI) includes the study of symbolic programming problem solving and search .

From the third human technological perspective reason view point, today's computer can do many well-defined tasks, for example, arithmetic operations, are much faster and more accurate than human beings. However, the computers' interaction with their environment is not very sophisticated yet. How can human test whether a computer has reached the general intelligence level of a human being? Can a computer convince a human interrogator that it is a human? But before thinking of such advanced kinds of machines, human will start developing our own extremely simple " intelligent" machines.

So, it is possible that human society job nature will to be changed to artificial intelligent society when (AI) technology is developed to the mature stage in the future.

● Why does human need artificial intelligence machines?
One of major division in (AI) is between humans who think (AI) is the only serious way of finding out how we (human) work and human who want companies to do very smart things, independently of how we (human) work. This is the important distinction between cognitive scientists vs engineers. One of another major division in (AI) is between symbolic (AI), which represents information through symbols and their relationships. Specific Algorithms are used to process these symbols to solve problems

or deduce new knowledge and connectionist. So (AI) , which represents information in network. Biological processes underlying learning, task performance and problem solving are imitated from human mind behaviors.

Thus, it is possible that artificial intelligence machines can do the better judgicious behavior to compare human.

● How does artificial intelligence influence future working changing in automation employment and productivity aspects?

In the automation changing influence aspect, as companies increasingly use robots on production lines or algorithms to optimize their logistics manage inventory, any carry out other core business functions. Technological advances are creating a new automation age in which ever-smarter and more flexible machines will be deployed on an ever larger scale in the marketplace. However, researching artificial intelligence with how influences human working nature. We need to answer these questions: How will automation transform the workplace? What will the implications for employment? And what is likely to be its impact both on productivity in the global economy and on employment?

Advances in robotics, artificial intelligence, and machine learning are growing in a new age of automation as machines match or outperform human performance in a range of work activities, including ones requiring cognitive capabilities. What factors are determined the changing in workplace adoption by artificial intelligence innovation? What advantages are automation? Automation of activities can be enabled businesses to improve performance by reducing errors and improving quality and speed, and achieving outcomes that go beyond human capabilities.

Some scientists indicated based on their scenario modeling. They estimated automation could raise producing growth globally by 0.8 to 1.4 percent annually. Almost, the activities people are paid almost $16 trillion in wages to do in global economy have the potential to be automated by adopting currently demonstrated technology. According to their analysis of more than 2,000 work activities across 800 occupations. When less than 5% of all occupations have of least 30% of activities that could be automated. They also indicated that technical economic and social factors will determine automation. Continued technical progress, for example, in areas such as natural language processing is a key factor beyond technical feasibility , the cost of technology, competition with labor including skills, and supply and demand dynamics, performance benefits including and beyond labor cost savings and social and regulatory acceptance will affect (alter) the scope of automation.

Other some scientists also indicate U.S. country for example, the anticipate shift in the activities in labor force of a similar order of magnitude as the long term sight away from agriculture and decreases in manufacturing. Share of employment in the United States both which were achieved. So, those factors can influence why artificial intelligence technology needs. So, it is possible that future agriculture and manufacturing both industries will apply (AI) technology manufacturer-kind of job nature to raise productivity instead of farmers, fruit picking workers, farming transportation labours as well as factory manufacturing workers and supervisors etc. human-kind of job nature.

● Is artificial intelligence possible to replace labor ?

Not just intelligence, but also debating, if machines are capable of having a conscious minds. Artificial intelligence has those characteristics as below:

On functionalism aspect, artificial intelligence inputs mental states, sensory inputs, (beliefs, desires being in pain feeling) and behavioral outputs. Since mental states are identified by a functional role, which are thoughts to be manifested in various systems. Even, perhaps computers which are physical devices with electronic substrate that inform computations on inputs to give outputs similar to brains which are artificial intelligence composed of part any intrinsic relationship to each other. Thus, artificial intelligence activities is not the whole itself, but into parts or on external influence on the parts.

On dualism aspect, artificial intelligence is a set of views about the relationship between mind are matter. On materialism aspect, it builds the only thing that exists is matter, including consciousness.

On biological naturalism aspect, it is similar a human brain than feels pains makes mental situation. So, artificial intelligence is similar biologist which might to be excited to human labor work.

Hence, it seems artificial intelligence can change (alter) or replace human labor work of nature in possible in the future.

● Can (AI) technology replace human labour nature of work?

On technological innovation reason view point, the history development of artificial intelligence studying the intelligence is one of most ancient scientific discipline. The history development of artificial intelligence what aims to achieve human use to sense, learn remember and think, logic probability, decision making and calculation develop from mathematics, instead of replacement human labor functions.

Artificial intelligence history development aim is the scientific analysis of skills in connection and practice with the appearance of computers from 1950 year beginning. The artificial intelligence (AI) can deal with the ultimate challenges. How can (either biological or electronic) mind sense, understand and manipulate a world that is much simple and more complex than itself? And what if would human like to construct something with such capabilities?

The general-purpose software of the early period of (AI) were only able to solve simple tasks effectively and failed when which should be used in a wider range or an more difficult tasks. One of the sources of difficulty was that early software had very few or mix knowledge about the problems which handled, and activities successes by simply syntactic manipulation. Moreover, the other difficulty was that many problems that were tried to solve by the (AI) were untreatable.

The early (AI) software whether trying step sequences based on the basic facts about the problem that should be solved, experimented with different combinations till which found a solution. From the end the 1960 year, developing the so-called expert systems were emphasized. These systems had (sue-based) knowledge base about the field which handled. Till to the beginning of the 1970 year, (Prolog) the logical programming language was born, which was built in the computation realization of a version of the resolution calculus. (Prolog) is a remarkably prevalent tool in developing expert systems (on medical, judiciary and other scopes), but natural language parsers were implemented in this language. Then, in 1981 s, the Japanese announced the fifth generation computer system project, a 10 years plan to build an intelligent computer system that use the (Prolog) language as a machine code. Nowadays, (AI) can be applied any industries, such as car manufacturing industry can use (AI) technological machine-men manufacture car, instead of replacing human labors in factory. Even, in the future, using (AI) machine-men drivers can drive any private cars or public transportation tools, instead of replacing human drivers, e.g. bus, train, tram, ferry etc. Also in the future, machine-men can replace housewives to serve families to do housekeeping clean job , e.g. cleaning toilets, bathrooms, kitchens, even cooking functions at home. So (AI) machine-man can reduce housewives works at home. Moreover, (AI) machine man can take care old people , when who are living at homes or elder care centers.

So, it seems artificial intelligence (AI) will be possible developed to manufacture a new generation machine-man to assist (serve) families to do any simply cleaning or cooking jobs at homes. Moreover, the overall demand of (AI) general social needs will also rise, such as security, driving transportation tools, restaurant cleaning, elder centers care service etc. So, it seems that individual or families or social needs of (AI) will be increase in the future. Thus, it will influence macro economy growth (GDP) if there are large house family consumer group and hotel or bus or taxis or ferry etc. different business consumer group demand any artificial intelligence machine numbers increasing. Then, the artificial intelligence products and material manufacturers must need to buy many artificaial intelligence materials to produce any kinds of artificial intelligence machines to prepare to satisfy consumer individual needs. Consequently, macro economy will grow to the owned artificial intelligence development countries, e.g. US, China, UK.

● Why can artificial intelligence satisfy human needs?

First, On machine-man satisfactory demand aspect view point, it makes computers that think, it is the automation of activities. We associate with human thinking: like decision making, learning. It is the act of creating machine that perform function that require intelligence when performed by people. It is the study of mental faculties through the use of computational models. It is the study of computations that make it possible to perceive, reason and act. It is a branch of computer science that is concerned with the automation of intelligent behavior. It is anything in computing service that human don't yet know how to do property.

Second, on thought aspect artificial intelligence means systems thank think like humans, systems that think rationally.

Third, on behavioral aspect, artificial intelligence systems that act like human and that systems act rationally. However, the basic objective of (AI) is to represent human's thought processes in computation . These machines are supposed to exhibit behavior that. It is performed by a human being, would be considered intelligent. However, some authors feel (AI) has disadvantages, such as it is not creative, it is excited in the use of sensory devices, it can't make use of a very wide context of experiences and it does not use common sense.

For speech recognition and understanding function needs example, (AI) can be applied in speech recognition and understanding function, which (AI) speech or voice recognition is a data input method. For example, the computer recognizes and understands one (or a few) word commands. Speech understanding on the other hand is the computer's ability to understanding a spoken language. That is , the computer understands the meaning of sentences, an paragraphs through (AI).

So, (AI) can be attempted to learn human language how to speak. It is similar to translate human language skill, instead of actual human speaking skill. Also, (AI) can assist handicap learning or language student how to listen different languages by machine-man sounds from computers more accurately.

So, it seems that it (AI) can replace human language teachers speaking function and can change teaching language nature of job in language speaking and listening education industry.

● Is artificial intelligence one good choice for human future technological benefit?

Nowadays, new technology development is popular. However, artificial intelligence is one kind of new technology choice among different technologies innovation. So it brings this question: Is artificial intelligence technology value to invest? To answer this question. I shall indicate some other new technology developments to compare (AI) technology development to judge which has urgent needs to achieve human expectation nowadays.

For example, why is green peace interested in new technologies? New technologies features prominently in our ongoing campaigns against genetic modified crops and number power. However, which are also an integral part of our solutions to environmental challenges, including renewable energy technologies, such as solar, wind and wave (water) power energy as well as waste treatment technologies, such as mechanical, biological treatment.

It seems humans need concern how to apply (AI) technology to solve environment pollution challenges in our future. So, environment protective, agriculture, natural energy technology will be popular demand to attempt to apply (AI) technology to solve their challenges or apply (AI) to assist to develop their industry.

What is relationship between (AI) and economy growth

● How can artificial intelligence technology influence economy?
Advances in artificial intelligence (AI) technology and related fields have opened up new markets and new opportunities progress in critical areas, such as health, education, energy, economic development, social welfare and the environment pollution.

(AI) automation will continue to create wealth and expand the global economy development in the future. However, when many will benefits that growth won't be costless and will be accompanied by changes in the skills, that workers need to increase productivity in the economy and structural changes in the economy. So, in the skills that workers need to succeed in the economy and structural changes.

I shall indicate why aggressive policy action will be needed to help Americans who are disadvantaged by these changes , due to (AI) technology is caused. For automation industry change example, artificial intelligence (AI) capabilities will enable automation of some tasks that have long required human labor. These artificial intelligence technology introduction can increase new opportunities for individuals. The economy and society, but (AI) has also the potential to disrupt be current livelihoods of many Americans. However, (AI) leads to unemployment and increase in inequality over the long run depends not only on the (AI) technology itself, but also on the institutions and policies that are changed.

Thus, it is possible that (AI) technology will raise some countries unemployment number if the employer apply (AI) technology workers to work instead of human labor in their factories, but it can also raise productivities for these employers.

● Can (AI) influence global economy growth?

Technological progress is main driver of growth of GDP per capita, allowing output to increase faster than labor and capital . However, technology can increase productivity, but also decrease the number of labor hours needed to create a unit of output. So (AI) causes unequal to labor wage decreases, even reduces the number of labor to manufacture, e.g. artificial intelligence technology of automation car manufacturing industry; clothing manufacturing industry; plane manufacturing etc. high technology of artificial intelligence manufacturing method. But (AI) should be potential environment benefit, although it raises unemployment ratio. Moreover, it can rise production , due to many skilled craft were replaced by the combination of machines and lower-skilled labor. The result of (AI) technology introduction , it causes output per hour risen when inequality declined, driving up average living standards, but the labor of some high-skill workers was no longer as valuable in the market. Otherwise, if (AI) technology is continue developed to be success. Some routine intensive occupations will be loss, which focused on predictable, e.g. easily programmable tasks, such as switchboard operators, filing clerks, travel agents, and assembly line workers would be particularly replaced by new (AI) technology. However, at the same time, (AI) technology development will bring these benefits: improvement in education (training (AI) technology scientists) , due to (AI) manufacturing technology needs are raising to businesses and institutional changes, such as the reduction in unionization and raising in the minimum wage to the (AI) manufacturing technology skilled labor in factories.

Because (AI) technology is not a single technology, but rather a collection of technologies that are applied to specific tasks, the effects of (AI) will be felt unevenly though the economy. It will bring some tasks will be most easily automated than others , and some jobs will be affected more than others, both negatively and positively. Finally, new jobs are likely to be directly created in areas , such as the development and supervision of (AI) as well as indirectly created in a range areas though out the economy as higher incomes lead to expanded demand.

However, if (AI) technology could dominate global labor markets. If labor productivity increases, do not influence into wage increases, then the large economic gains brought about by (AI) technology could be increased wealth inequality, due to employers can reduce production cost, but workers (labors) wages will not be increased, even will be decreased. Hence, it seems the (AI) technology will bring disadvantages to labor market to cause unemployment or reduce wages in possible, although it can reduce employer individual salary (wage) expenditure and it can raise productivity.

● How can artificial intelligence impact global economy growth?
Artificial intelligence (AI) technology is a branch of computer science that aims to create intelligent machines that work and react like humans. So, (AI) is a technology that appears to impact (influence) human preference by learning, understanding complex contents, enhancing humans in executing both routine and non-routine tasks. In the future, (AI) technology that can be virtual personal assistant, as well as it may exist, such as robots with human-like processing capabilities.

How can (AI) technology impact global economy growth over the next 10 years? During this time period, (AI) technology is predicted to have wide-ranging applications including: Machine learning that automates analytical model building by using algorithms that allow machines to operate without human assistance.

In global education aspect, potential applications include predicting cause-and-effect relationships from biological data, identifying new drugs, self-driving cars, and protecting against fraud, improved natural language processing that allows computers to continue to better analysis, understand and generate language to interface with humans using natural human languages. For example, transcribing notes dictated by physicians, automatically drafting articles and translating text and speech. So (AI) technology can be applied to education aspect to improve humans' knowledge level.

In visual art aspect, (AI) machine vision that allows computers to identify objects, scenes and activities in images. Current applications of (AI) machine vision include providing objective descriptions for the blind seeing(visual) needs.

We except the economic effects of (AI) technology to include both direct GDP growth from sectors that develop or manufacture. (AI) technology and indirect GDP growth through increased productivity in existing sectors that employ some form of (AI). If (AI) technology is an increasingly critical component of more products, it will become an integral part of many people's lives. Thus, (AI)'s ability to influence economic activity, rather than the economic or development status of the region. (AI) has the potential to impact income classes and to bring significant gains to both developed and developing countries. For example, (AI) has the potential to optimize good production around the world by analyzing agricultural regions and identifying what is necessary to improve crop yields.

In estimating the future economic effects by (AI) technology innovation, it is important to note that it is challenging to accurately predict which applications of (AI) will ultimately be commercially successful. In micro level economic influence, we need to apply methodologies to estimate the economic effects of investment in firms developing (AI) technology since investment levels in a technology are a telling sign of the future potential of that (AI) technology.

● How can (AI) influence GDP of high income countries in the next ten years?

How (AI)'s development may affect the global economy over the next ten years. In fact, (AI) technology has the potential to affect business across the global in a wide range of industries in ways only a number of technologies have done in the parts. For example, (AI) technology's expected to be a useful tool for enhancing human capabilities and in some instances replacing functions, such as driving a car, adoption of broadband internet, mobile telephone, industrial robotic automation have served to enhance human capabilities.

However, significant public debate has focused on projections of (AI) technology's effect on the labor force. However, large companies prefer to invest in (AI) technological industry. For example, face book's (AI) research lab., google machine intelligence lab. and micro soft machine learning and artificial intelligence research division are all making advances in (AI) technology and investing in the industry's top talent. Additionally, between 2010 year and 2015 year, nearly $5 billion in venture capital funding invested in firms across the global developing and employing (AI) technology (Facebook (AI) Research).

● How can artificial intelligence impact on workplace?

Modern information technologies and the labor economy growth of machines is powered by artificial intelligence have already strongly influenced the world of work in the 21 ST century. Computers, algorithms and software simplify every tasks and it is impossible to image how most of our life could be managed without them. How can be the information economy characterized by exponential growth replaces the most production industry based on economy of scales? What will the future world of work look like and how long will it take to get? Will the future world of work be a world where humans spend less time earning their livelihood? Alternatively, are mass unemployment, mass poverty and social distortions also possible scenario for the future, where robots, artificial intelligence systems play an increasingly central role? These questions concern how artificial intelligence further development . Can influence labor economy growth on workplace ? When the labor market has widespread impact on intelligence property, information technology, product liability, competition and labor and employment laws.

How (AI) technology impacts on labor workplace.

The future influence any organizations how labor economies use of (AI) can be analyzed, such as deep machine learning is based on a set of model high level data. Unlike human workers, the machines are connected the whole time in workplace. If one machine makes a mistake, all autonomous systems will keep this in mind and will avoid the same mistake the next time.

Over the long run intelligent machines will win against every human expert. Production robots have been replacing employees because of the (AI) technology. They work more precisely than humans and cost loss. Creative solutions like 3D printers and the self learning ability of these production robots will replace human workers, the automatic data recording and data processing, traditional back office activities are no longer in demand. Autonomous software will collect necessary information and will send it to the employee who needs it. Additionally, dematerialization leads to the phenomenon that traditional physical products are becoming software. For example, CD or DVDs are being replaced by streaming services. The replacement of traditional event ticket, e-travel ticket service products or hard cash will be the next step, due to the possibility of payment by smartphone. So, (AI) technology will impact human's daily life consumption behaviors in the future. For another example, transportation tools, such as boats and ferries and private vehicles will use sensors and navigating without human input. Taxi and truck drivers will become obsolete, the stock store applies to stock managers and postal carriers of the delivery is distributed by (AI) machine delivery method.

What is the relationship between (AI) and (CRM)?

● Can (AI) technology impact on customer relationship management

(CRM) ?

Nowadays , (AI) is a technology almost as old as the computer industry itself, it is similar with the advent of personal assistants function to businesses and personal promotion channel, such as (Amazon's Alexa, Apple's Siri, Google's Assistant) image recognition (face book), personalized recommendations (Netflix , Amazon). Those innovations have been driven by a increase in processing power, lower cost hardware, and the exploding creation and availability of data. It seems, (AI) technology can impact global customer service management method.

How to forecast economic impact modeling to (AI) will affect global economy? Can human forecast business revenue growth and job creation (or destruction) based on (AI) applied to customer relationship management (CRM) activities? In addition to the economic impact on (AI) or (CRM) which can include an estimate of the economic impact attributable to sales forces customer base. What can economic benefits be brought to (CRM) from (AI) technology?

Artificial intelligence(AI) comprises a set of technologies that use natural language processing, machine learning, knowledge graphs, and other tools to answer questions, discover insights and provide recommendations. Computer systems can use (AI) hypothesize and formulate possible answers based on available evidence can be trained through the ingestion of vast amounts of content, and automatically adapt and learn from (AI) self mistakes and failures.

So, any business organizations (customer service departments) can provide efficient and effective customer relationship management of excellent customer service quality if which applied (AI) technology system. The different type of (AI) systems include: (AI) system platforms, machine learning (AI) based data preparation and enrichment tools, machine vision/ image recognition, voice speech recognition, text analysis and natural language processing, bots , e.g. face book website and virtual digital assistance solutions, social media pattern analysis , sentiment analysis, advanced numerical analysis (e.g. IOT streaming , machine logs), supporting technologies, knowledge base dialog management, Q&A processing etc. different (AI) technology system customer relationship management (CRM) tools.

(AI) (CRM) of activity can include these categories, such as: corporate marketing, marketing operation, field marketing, customer support, digital commerce, customer analytics, customer influenced product or service design, product or service pricing, finance information, presentation, customer billing, inventory , logistics and fulfilment support, partner management etc. different CRM tools.

(AI) technology of CRM has been carrying on plan different stages to achieve CRM personal assistant tool for businesses. The stages are such as, in the beginning stage of (AI) projects in place, implement now, pilot phase next year in the final stage of (AI) customer relationship management tools are foreseeable future. So, this CRM technology has been improved to plan in different stages every year to prepare to achieve full capacity of CRM service quality for businesses to use in the future.

Hence, how to develop an estimate prediction of the economic impact (AI) technologies could have CRM activities, which depends on gathering macroeconomic information on business revenue and the basic marketing of business revenue and the basic markup of business expenses by major functions (customer support, marketing and sales , production etc.)

An economic impact model that can gather data together and forecast the results how (AI) artificial intelligence technology brings (CRM) customer relationship management benefits to businesses, e.g. surveys investigation includes IT spending by sample countries, GDP and population estimates and forecasts, revenue per employee and ratios of IT spend to GDP. Surveys (questionnaire questions) of forecast results are influenced by (AI) impact can include: results are projected from surveys and rely on estimates are made by respondents on the expected financial improvements in categories of (AI) –assisted customer relationship management activities. The forecast assumes that these estimates are correct; financial estimates are based on estimates of "first year" improvement from full (AI) implementation; forecasts are from planning to implement any artificial intelligence of customer relationship management (CRM) projects, the improvement forecast is of categories of activity , e.g. corporate marketing , digital commerce, and customer analytics. They are not estimates of ROI for the (AI) software. They rely on conservative estimates to which each of these entities might affect company revenue, expenses or productivity. They also rely on estimates of the penetration of software in customer relationship management activities . Net new jobs created are based on the ratio of new revenue to jobs required to support that revenue . They can assume that 50% of the net new revenue will support increases in labor and the rest will go for capital and other operating expenses that may replace jobs lost to automation.

In the future, some of the ways in micro economic benefits to any organizations. (AI) technology is expected to impact CRM activities include: Spending up sales cycles, improving lead generation and qualification solving customer support problems faster (raising service quality), helping companies improve brand campaigns and recognition, lowering costs of support calls when increasing resolution rates, lowering the cost of recruiting employees and partners, increasing revenue from optimized product marketing, optimizing price, distribution logistics and preventing loss through fraud detection. So, micro economic benefits view point, it seems that (AI) CRM technology can raise any companies economic benefits for care term.

Artificial intelligence enables machines or the in-build software to behave like human beings which allows these decisions and act. The advent of (AI) is leading , talking, making decisions and act. The advent of (AI) is leading to new technologies advances and transforming the economic and employment opportunities for humans in a positive way. (AI) related technologies can facilitate our live. For example, industrial robotics, robotic medical assistants, smart games, financial forecasting software, big data analysis, algorithms in health and bioinformatics, pilotless cargo places, drone ambulances and general purpose and workplace robots and others. (Disruptors technologies: Advances that will transform life, business and the global economy).

Artificial intelligence also known as computational intelligence is defined as " the human –like intelligence exhibited by machines or software. It is theorized that intelligence of humans can be described and intelligence machines or software can simulate it. These machines software can be reasonable , learn, perceive and process information, like human mind and thus facilitate human life. They can think and act for us. So, artificial intelligence is an interdisciplinary field of study including computer science, neuroscience, psychology, linguistics and philosophy.

However, (AI) research and developments have economically impacted many industries, such as robotics, telecommunications, computer applications , health, finance, heavy manufacturing, transportation, aviation, e-service and e-commerce, military , music and movie, toys and games entertainment etc. industries.

In fact, many ideas, systems and technologies have been developing in the world of (AI) technology. However, which are net called or considered (AI) products, rather which are mentioned with their specific names, such as smart graphics, machine learning, e-commerce etc. (i.e. this is called (AI) effect).

● How can (AI) technology influence digital economy?

Nowadays, (AI) related industrial applications will replace most human power in fields, including call centers, customer services and air cargo transportation. (AI) technologies also help weather forecasting based on repeated rainfall pattern (data) recognition, through robotics (i.e. floor cleaning, moving lawns etc.) transporting people and products with unmanned vehicles, sending space unmanned smart shuttles, developing robotic arms, predicting market values in stock exchanges by internet, making homes safer, helping elderly and disabled using robotic servants etc.

Among the (AI) related technologies , there are a few that significance for the impact on society and especially on digital economy . (AI) is particularly influential in machine learning. Such as robotics, transportation, finance, health and bioinformatics, e-commerce , e-games, big online data gathering and internet-of-things. For example, machine e-learning is based in bioinformatics and robots that can learn new skills for better caregiving in healthcare. What is machine e-learning? Machines can e-learn from e-data gathering, coming up generalizations and making decisions to act in certain ways from internet.

There are important applications , such as e-machine perception, electronic online natural language learning processing, online search engines, online bioinformatics, online brain –computer interface, online game playing, online robot locomotion, online advertising, online computations finances, online health monitoring, online DNA classification and decision making, online in chemistry –cheminformatics . So, online machine learning can positively impact productivity and it can enhance information and analytical system from (AI) online channel.

What is robotics? Robotics is one of the most strongly influenced fields in (AI). For example, heavy manufacturing industries, robots and used and man power is replaced for effectiveness, precision, and accuracy, especially in respective or dangerous tasks, including welding, assembling , picking and placing .

So, robots can acquire new skills or adapt the changing dynamic environment. Also, artificial intelligence can be applied in developing transportation. For example, automated vehicles, driver assistance systems

, safety systems, collision avoidance systems and public transportation. Moreover, (AI) technology has proven to produce some of the best tools to predict stock market fluctuations from internet data gathering method. It's predictions are based on ever-evolving predictions algorithms and systems learn new models and make connections between historical data and new data to measure stock market trading more accurate from internet data gathering channel.

In health field, especially in health data processing , analysis, decision making support and medical diagnosis. So, online data can show which patients will need what treatment and what alternative drugs could be used more accurate from (AI) online data gathering method. Bioinformatics is an interdisciplinary field combining statistics, (AI) online technology can help in discovering data patterns and modeling through the application of machine learning, artificial neural networks and genetic algorithms. For example, further (AI) technology development of human genome project of online data sequences.

Online shopping can be facilitated by virtual assistants developed through (AI) technology and these assistants can offer the best advice. (AI) online purchase coming after every product image recommendations and personalization bring important revenue to shopping online sites, like Amazon . Smart computer graphics and games, artificial intelligence is useful in smarter computer, graphics, scene modeling , scene rendering processes in order to create, for example, effective human –robot interactions , online machine learning, online strategic games techniques etc. online computer related (AI) software.

So, online big data analysis and big data does have a critical need in the world of online intelligence machines and software in our future. In other words, (AI) offers online technology to enable online big data analysis to provide industrial organizations with valuable information for effective decision making in short time. For example, what IBM's Watson achieved: this machine used 200 million of structured and unstructured content with a special technology of hypothesis generation, massive evidence gathering, analysis and scoring from internet channel.

Finally, (AI) online technology another related internet invention (internet of things) (IOT) is the network of machines or objects connected through internet. These connected objects can sense their internal and external environment, communicate with each other, can send critical data and finally can make decisions to act or correct their environment from (AI) online technology. For example, factories can monitor and automatically change production processes, hospitals can monitor and regulate the health conditions of their patients , schools can collect data from facilities and cars can send data to car makers from (AI) online technology.

Partner predicts that (IOT) market will create about trillion amount value by 2020 year. Although machines collect big data from their environment, whether which gain an insight or learn from these online data largely depends on the (AI) online machine learning principals and (AI) online technology. In 2013, Mckinsey estimated that disruptive technologies closely related with potential economic impact in 2025 year between $7.1 to $13.1 trillion amount (automation of knowledge work, advanced robotics, autonomous or near-autonomous vehicles).

What is the relationship between
(AI) and global digital economy development ?

● Could work activities in China be automated
making in the nation with the world's largest automation potential?
Can (AI) technology influence China economy? Could China workers be affected and jobs made up of routine work activities and predictable? Will programmable tasks be particularly impact to China employment market ? When impact on labor market is likely to be gradual at the aggregate level, it can be sudden and dramatic at the level of specific work activities, rending some job obsolete fairly. Overall (AI) technology will raise digital skills when reducing demand for medium incomer inequality for China workers. It seems (AI) technology's effect on productivity could be crucial to China's future economic growth as the population ages are increasing.
In China, some biggest technological companies driving significant investments in research and development. Moreover, China is one of the leading global (AI) technology development county. However, China will need to focus on building its innovation capacity. For example, United States and United Kingdom are currently producing more influential (AI) technological research. However, if China planed to achieve (AI) technology success, it's traditional industries will need to develop technical know-how —to and overcoming implementation costs prepare to develop (AI) . When (AI) technology is introduced into China society, China government needs to raise concerning ethical, legal, technological security etc. business questions. Also, surrounding issues include privacy, discrimination, legal liability and regulation. It aims to encourage overseas

investors to choose to invest (AI) technological industry to raise GDP growth and manufacturing industries income growth for long term in China. If China encouraged overseas (AI) technology investment in its country. It is possible to influence China employment market to be changed. Because (AI) technology will impact to influence China people daily life. Due to (AI) technology is introduced to China society, many rich people will prefer to spend to buy any high (AI) technological products for entertainment or learning or machine man driving etc. daily necessity activities. Then it will raise GDP growth and will raise (AI) manufacturers or related-(AI) technological manufacturers profit. It is beneficial to China because it can become one high knowledgeable and (AI) technological economical society. But it will bring bad influences to raise unemployment chance for the low skillful labor. In labor economy aspect influence , how (AI) technology can influence China low skillful labor unemployment ratio raising. The raising low skill labor unemployment reason is because China low skillful human labors are argued or are replaced by (AI) technology creating new challenges to introduce to influence China society of simply human manufacturing job nature to be changed to be high (AI) technology manufacturing job nature in any China factories. Moreover, when (AI) technology introduction to China, it will cause other related social challenges in China. The varied (AI) related challenges, including the difficulty of creating safe and reliable hardware for sensing and affecting (transportation and education), the challenges of gaining public trust, a low resource comities and public safety and security, the challenges of overcoming fears or marginalizing humans in China employment and workplace and the risk of diminishing interpersonal trust because the low skillful labors won't believe any China employers will give chance to employ them , due to (AI) technology will replace their skills and man manufacturing of productivity is much less to compare to (AI) technology manufacturing method.

● How does (AI) technology influence
the future of employment change?
Are future nature of jobs changed to computerization from (AI) technology? Where are the probability of computing occupations from (AI) technology influence? What is expected impacts of future computing on labor market from (AI) technology influence? John Maynard Keynes's frequently cited prediction of widespread technological unemployment " du to our discovery of means of economic the use of labor outrunning the pace

of which we can find new used of labor" (Keynes, 1933, p.3).

In the future, (AI) technology will impact some nature of occupations to change computing. This chance will also influence some countries' economic change. For example, some factory human labors hand routine manufacturing tasks will be changed to computerization of routine manufacturing tasks by (AI) technological machine men hand manufacturing method. it will cause a structured shift in the labor market, with workers reallocating their labor supply from middle-income manufacturing to low-income service occupations.

Arguably, this is because the manual tasks of service occupations are less computerization, as who require a higher degree of flexibility and physical adaptability. So, (AI) technology will influence the human hand labor skillful occupation nature of task cheaper , such as vehicle manufacturing , ship manufacturing, computer manufacturing, steel manufacturing, television, radio etc. home electronic products of heavy machine industry change. Due to (AI) technology machine man will be proper to be used to manufacturing these electronic products when the (AI) technology innovation can develop to the mature stage. Then, any countries manufacturers will choose to use (AI) technology machine man, instead of human hand production.

Supposing the future prices of computing are fallen, seriously, problem solving skills are becoming relatively productive, explaining the substantial employment growth in manufacturing occupations, involving cognitive tasks where skilled labor has a comparative advantage, as well as the increase education needs for (AI) technology computing of machine man subject study.

Prediction of education needs for (AI) technology student numbers will increase, due to manufacturing industry needs many (AI) technology students in future employment market. Another (AI) technology influence if the future (AI) technological innovation, e.g. machine man manufacturing or machine man service industries will both increase demand, then with more sophistic software technologies will be disrupted labor markets by marketing workers redundant.

For publishing industry, what is striking about the case in paper book publishing industry will be unpopular? Due to the electronic book publishing industry will be popular, e.g. Amazon publish . (AI) technology can influence paper book manufacturing method which is replaced by machine man electronic book manufacturing method as well as it will cause the computerization is no longer confined to routine manufacturing tasks. Due to (AI) machine man manufacturing technology will be proper to be used to manufacture any products in short time efficiently and effectively , e.g. electronic book products. In the future, if it is fact to occur this case, such as (AI) technological machine man manufacturing method will be adopted (applied) to manufacture electronic books or any products in possible. (AI) technology will cause many manufacturing workers are unemployed. It is beneficial to employers, who can reduce to spend much wages expenditure to employ manufacturing workers, but it will cause many manufacturing workers loss jobs and reduce income to support whose families lives. It will cause social challenges, e.g. increasing stealing crimes if the manufacturing workers had not other skills to find other jobs to do easily. So, manufacturers need to concern over technological unemployment which will be hardly future phenomenon if who decided to dismiss all manufacturing workers, due to (AI) technology machine men replace to them.

If (AI) technology can be innovated to produce any kinds of machine man to serve any service or manufacturing industries successfully. Then, it will bring these questions: Can future that workers be influenced to be automation employment and productivity by (AI) technology influence? Does it impact to influence the (AI) technology countries' productivity and growth and natural resources development and labor markets and evolution of global financial markets and economic impact of technology and innovation and urbanization etc. issues? How will automation transform the workplace? What will be the implication for employment? What is likely to be its impact both on productivity in the global economy and on employment?

In fact, automatic of activities can enable businesses to improve performance by reducing errors chance and improving quality and speed, and same cases achieving outcomes that go beyond human capabilities. Some economists indicate (AI) technology would give a needed boost to economic growth and prosperity have of the working age population in many countries. Based on the scenario modeling, they estimate automation could raise productivity growth globally by 0.8 to 1.4 % annually. They also indicated that almost half the activities people are almost $1.6 trillion in wages to do in the global economy have the potential to be automated adapting current demonstrates technology, according to their analysis of more than 2,000 work activities across 800 occupations. When less than

5% of all occupations can be automated entirely using demonstrated technology, about 60% of all occupations have at least 30% of worker made activities, that would be automated. More occupation will change to be automated. They also indicated for business performance benefits of automation are relatively clear, but the issues are more complicated by policy making to attract foreign investors. Beyond technical feasibility, the cost of technology, competition labor will include skills and supply and demand dynamics, performance benefits and beyond labor cost savings and social and regulatory acceptance will affect the automation. Their predictions suggest that half of today work activities could be automated by 2055 year, but this could happen 10 to 20 years earlier or latter depending on the various factors in addition to their wider economic condition.

Some scientists suggest (AI) technology is finally starting to deliver real-life business benefits. Computer power is growing significantly , algorithms are becoming more sophisticated and perhaps most important of all, the world is generating vast quantities of the fuel that powers (AI) technology data billions of gigabytes of it every day. Also, online firms are digital natives, such as Google online search service company is investing on (AI) technology. For new though most of the news if coming from the suppliers of (AI) technologies. And many new users are only in the experimental phase. Few products are on the market or are likely to arrive these soon to drive immediate and widespread adoption. As a result, analysts believe (AI) technology's potential will give true economic benefit in the future. (AI) industry will introduce to suppliers and users to raise economic potential of (AI) technology.

In the future, (AI) technology systems can solve business problems. Some scientists categorized those into five technology systems that are key areas of (AI) technology development: robotics and autonomous vehicles, computer vision language virtual agents and machine learning , which is based on algorithms that learn from data without replying on rules-based programming in order to draw conclusions or direct an action.

Such as computer vision and language includes natural language processing, analytics, speech recognition technology, some are about learning from information, such as about machine learning and others are related to acting on information, such as robotics, autonomous vehicles and virtual agents, which are computer programs that can converse with humans. Machine learning and a subfield called deep learning are artificial intelligence applications.

● Can artificial intelligence impact global economy growth?

Artificial intelligence (AI) is a term first defined in 1956 year. It is a branch of computer science that aims to create intelligent machines that work and react like humans. In contrast today, 60 years later, (AI) is characterized by a number of applications, including computers playing games against humans and understanding human languages, virtual personal assistants, and robotics which involve computers seeing , hearing and reacting to sensory stimuli. In the future, technologists predict for (AI) technology ranging from (AI) being used as a tool to aid relatively simple processes for robots with human like mental capabilities, who expect (AI) technology can emulate human performance by learning, coming to mind its own conclusions, understanding complex content, engaging in dialog with people, enhancing human cognitive performance or replacing humans in executing both routine and non-routine tasks. In existing industry, (AI) technology is used , such as targeted advertising and virtual used personal assistant as well as the (AI) technology that my exist in the future, such as robots with human vehicle processing capabilities.

The range of (AI) technology's progress in the future will determine the economic impact future of (AI) technology on the global economy with more limited advances and applications (i.e. weak (AI) only) corresponding to more limited economic impacts and more substantial progress, i.e. strong (AI) technology is corresponding to more significant economic impact.

(AI) technology learning that automates analytical model, including predicting cause-and-effect relationship from biological data, identifying new drugs, self-driving cars and protecting against fraud etc. functions. Also (AI) learning can improve natural language processing that allows computers to continue to better analyze, understand and generate language to interface with human using the natural human language, virtual personal assistant, helps users by providing scheduling appointment, reminds organizing personal finance and finding providers of various services, machine vision allows (AI) machine man to identify object, scenes and activities in detect pedestrians and bicyclists.

We expect the economic effects of (AI) technology to include both direct GDP growth from sectors that develop or manufacture (AI) technology and indirect GDP growth through increased productivity in existing sectors that employ some from of (AI) technology. If (AI) producing sectors could grow, then it could lead to increase revenues and employment of (AI) technological professionals within these existing firms as well as the potential creation of entirely new economic activities to any countries' societies productivity improvement in existing sectors could be realized through faster and move efficient processes and decision making as well as increased (AI) technological knowledge and access to information available in societies easily.

In the future, if (AI) technology is an increasingly critical component of more products, it will become an integral part of necessary products of many people's lives. The extent of (AI)'s economy effort is also likely to vary from region to region, thought variation may be more dependent on the predominate economic activity of a region and the (AI) ability can influence economic activity, rather then the economic or developmental status of the regions. (AI) technology can move accessibility and can use source development to do international business between one country and another country.

So (AI) technology has the potential to give benefits to different income chooses and to bring significant gains to both developed and developing countries. For agricultural technology, (AI) has the potential to optimize food production around the world by analyzing agricultural regions and identifying what is necessary to improve crop yield. In total, (AI) technology gives greater economic impact to any countries agricultural regions if which implemented (AI) technology to grow crop , fruit etc. food production in the farms.

Investment in (AI) technology is such as capital investment to any countries' public or private enterprises. So, it will have large economic impact to the future . If the (AI) technology is reasonable invested to the different needs aspect by the public or private enterprises in the country. Then, it will have good economic impact to the country in the future. However, when (AI) technology is likely to affect both the productivity and employment components of economic growth in many sectors. Significant public debate has focused on projections of (AI)'s effect on the labor force. However, for instance, some researchers have argued that the rise of (AI) technology and automation will led to significant unemployment as capital is substituted for the low skillful labor. So, they point to the concern that the increasing sophistication of (AI) technology may balance skilled and semi-skilled workers and the reduce the size of the middle class. However, this is not a new argument, due to (AI) technology negatively affecting the labor force and leading to mass unemployment. Because the (AI) technology is the substitution of machinery for human labor. Although, employment in certain industries, has been reduced in the past due to technological advancement. For long term, the labor market has adapted to the introduction of new technology, giving rise to new jobs in new areas. (AI) technology may also be accomplished without a reduction to total employment in the long-term to some Asia countries, such as Hong Kong and Japan. Because Hong Kong and Japan many low skilled labor, e.g. security, cleaner who complaint that employers need them to work long time hours. (abnormal working hours) e.g. one day 12 to 15 working hour per day. Hence, if (AI) machine means invention technology success. Security or cleaning job can be worked from (AI) machine man in some hours every day in order to reduce the long time working hours cleaners or security workers, e.g. one (AI) machine man works 4 hours for cleaning or security job, one day as well as another cleaner or security labor only needs to work 8 hours one day. So total security or cleaning employers can employ 12 hours machine cleaners or security workers and human cleaners or security workers in one day. For long term benefit, Hong Kong or Japan every security or cleaning worker does not need to work 12 hours minimum working hours one day. They won't feel tried and bore and without private with whose families, so who will accept to do these cleaning or security jobs, even they can raise work efficient and performance when who feel happy and health.

So, (AI) technology of machine man invention can raise low skillful labor efficiency and it can help them to avoid abnormal working hours demand in some busy work life countries, such as Hong Kong and Japan. Before, one Japan female labor feel unhappy to work, due to who often needs to work abnormal working hours for her employer and who has less sleeping and without any private time to enjoy her life with her families every day. So this abnormal working hours factor causes her to do commit suicide behavior, then she is die unlucky. So (AI) technology of machine man invention ought avoid abnormal working hours demand for employer in any countries in the future.

The most important occurrence to any employers, some researchers had attempted to do one experiment to find that private research and development , venture capital and public research and development investment all have strong net effect or economic growth with venture capital funding further having the strongest such effect from (AI) technology. The researchers hypothesize the venture capital investment contributes to economic growth through (AI) technology innovation and by the capacity of an economy to use existing (AI) technology knowledge to increase productivity. They predict the impacts of venture capital, business-research and development and public research and development can raise multi factor productivity from (AI) technology introduction.

Can (AI) technology influence the economic development to developing countries? The developing regions of the world contain most of natural resources. If one day, (AI) technology has invent one kind of machine man which can assist any gas or oil workers to seek any new oil/gas natural resource locations easily. I believe that (AI) technology can help these natural resource exploitation countries will gain economic benefit more easily. So, (AI) driven technology can be used to change to create any new opportunities to address poor management or resources and improve human well being, such as Africa Latin America and India can use (AI) technology machine man to seek any oil/gas natural resource countries exploitation activities to attempt to gain much economic benefits.

● Why will (AI) technology grow economic
development ?

Nowadays, increases in capital and labor are no longer driving the levels of economic growth, such as (AI) technology. The ability of increase in capital investment and in labor of traditional drivers of production, have no longer to be enjoyed in most developed economies ,e.g. developed country, US, UK . However, artificial intelligence has the potential to overcome the physical limitation of capital and labor to avoid missing out on this opportunity. So, policy makers and business leaders must prepare for and work toward a future with artificial intelligence. They must do with the idea that (AI) is another simply method to enhance productivity method . Rather they must see (AI) as the tool that can transform thinking about how growth is created.

Economists have always thought of new technologies are as driving growth their ability to enhancing. It can replace labor and capital factor of production. So, it brings this question: What is the factor of production (AI) technology characteristics. They key factor is to see (AI) technology as a capital-labor .

(AI) can replicate labor activities at much greater scale and speed, and to even perform some tasks began the capabilities of human. For example, by using virtual assistants , 1000 legal documents can be reviewed in a matter of days instead of taking three people six moths to complete. Some (AI) technology may be one kind of factor of production in the future. For another example, people will work in workplace digitalization environment. So, in the future, working environment and information management are automated. Such as Konica camera sale company will use workplace digitalization. So , (AI) technology can provide workplace digitalization in order to raise productivity efficiency. (AI) technology will be one kind of production which is replaced by workplace digitalization and it will grow any organization productivity efficiently. Then, (AI) technology will assist overall social economy growth , due to productivity is raised and products can be produced in short time to prepare to sell in consumption market. So, time will be shortened to increase GDP growth fast for the development of (AI) technology countries.

● How can (AI) technology impact to global
economic and social and psychological
changes?

What will be the development of (AI) technology and predictions concerning the future evolution? The computers and robots will develop conscious, intelligent and minds into humans, enhancing psychological and behavioral abilities and allowing for direct communication with (AI) minds. (AI) technology will be impacted human life by (AI) technology information communicative and environmental influence. A " world brain" and " world mind", this psychological system will be enhanced and enriched the capacities of both individual and collective cognition by (AI) technology of service industries.

(AI) technology with influence these human needs of service industries changes, such as , biological science, finance, entertainment, business, biological science, transportation, communication military etc. The personal computer evolution, the internet and the world wide web which exploded on the scene, linking business, homes, schools, social organizations which were a completely unpredicted phenomenon to influence human life. Kurzweil (1999) predicts that by 2029 year, most human communication will be with machines. According to Person, by 2100 year, there will be human machine convergence.

How can (AI) technology influence environmental protection to make benefits to farming economic growth? (AI) technology can be applied to predict how to solve environmental pollution challenge to avoid to damage any crop or vegetable or rice or fruit etc. food growth. Because environmental experts can gather global environmental pollution data from an environmental database to build a perform a systematic analysis from (AI) technology. The first step is this broad analysis can include understanding, statistical and data gathering techniques to obtain the relevant data, the correlation among the variables involved, and a list of possible models. The next step is to select a set of methods and models that cover all kinds of knowledge and functionalities needed for the decision making process. Once the models are selected, they must be fully implemented by means of machine learning , data mining, statistical or numerical technique. After that, those models must be integrated to build the whole EDSS. The EDSS must be tested to check its performance, accuracy, usefulness and reliability, both from the user's and (AI) technology/computer scientist's point of view. If these is any wrong feature in any development stage, such as model's integration, models' implementation, selection of models, database, problem analysis etc. the developers must come back in the update th required components. When the evaluation phase is all right, the EDSS is ready to be applied to the environment. The great contribution of artificial intelligence to EDSS the integration of several methods complementing the classical statistical models/simulation , statistical analysis, linear models, etc. and numerical models (control algorithms, optimization techniques etc.) .

This cooperation makes the resulting systems more reliable and powerful in coping with real world environment systems. Date interpretation has been a principal area of research in (AI) technology since the very beginning. The most demanding problem in the environmental assessment context. Knowledge representation permits the definition of the different types of data that the existing methods adapt to the process. There is also a lot of work to clean, repair and transform the huge available quantities of raw data. Apart from this, the availability of meta-information or background knowledge is required to guide the process. Data mining is multi-disciplinary: It covers expert systems, data based technology, statistics, data visualization and unsupervised machine learning. These techniques operate at the level of data and background information, where numerous and often incompatible new commensurate pieces of information from disparate sources have to be brought together (K, Fedra, 1994).

So, it seems that in the future, (AI) technology with the increasing maturity in particular those related to knowledge and engineering, new dimensions can be assisted to users in environmental decision making are available. For example, many environmental systems are characterized both by incomplete models and by limited data. Hence, in the future, (AI) technology will be applied to predict climate change to reduce crop or fruit etc. food agriculture challenge by climate change bad influence.

● Will (AI) technology influence digital economy change to manufacturing industry ?

To understand how the manufacturing business must adapt to prosper in the technology, we need to understand how (AI) technology will change us to shape our daily habits to satisfy our expectation of products to how we shop and even the immediate of the entire process. For example, taxi services are in the crosshairs as on demand transportation services like, available of the touch of a smart phone button expand. In fact, Yellow lab, US country , san Francisco city's largest taxi company is filing for bankruptcy as the industry starts to change faster than almost anyone expected. However, at this point, its more than an app that is changing, some our taxi passengers renting taxi transportation to catch consumption behavior.

(AI) technology will influence digital economy for taxi passenger's individual customer experience, offering a growing renting taxi to catch of service and feedback opportunities when any one taxi passenger who chooses to use mobile phone app online tool to prepaid to rent any taxi more easily.

Also in the long term, (AI) technology can influence vehicles drive themselves of behavior. Already, companies like Google and GM are working on projects to bring fleets of autonomous vehicles to cities at the path of a button.

Moreover, this on-demand service model is beginning to appear across a much broader range of markets. For example , Amazon company is investing in its own fleet of trucks, planes and even drone at the same time as it pushes for same-day delivery of products. As some point, vehicles will be autonomous too. So, it seems that (AI) technique will influence any transportations choose to use digital autonomous driving technology in the future . For Amazon company case, it is not stopping of logistics. It is also aiming to automatically manage the supply of consumer home products with its recently launched Amazon replenishment service, Dash. Dash is a digital service that enables that connected derive to automatically order physical products from Amazon when supplies are running low. So, it seems (AI) technology will be applied to logistic function by digital technology method introduction in the future.

Hence autonomous vehicles will optimize industry supply chains and logistics operations through increased efficiency and flexibility. In fact, fully automated and lean supply chains will keep reduce load sizes and inventory by leveraging smart distribution technologies and smaller autonomous vehicles by machine man assistance. If Amazon continues to grow market share for online sales by reducing effort required by the consumer to place an order, when also contributing the almost immediate delivery of products to the doorstep. So, it will further fuel the trend toward on-demand derive. As Amazon company fuels the on-demand economy, consumers will expect immediacy in more parts of the digital economy. On top of speed, consumers increasing expect more personalization options.
So, (AI) technology will influence digital manufacturing, such as Amazon publishing to monitor every aspect of every process in real -time and communicating to self-optimized deep learning robotics, new methods of high volume and high customization will become possible. Then, as products merge into product platforms and even services, manufacturers have the opportunity to provide components and platforms used by smaller players. So, (AI) technology will influence manufacturing industry to choose automated SMI lines, robots installed, automation engineers.

Another future (AI) technology development can be applied to space science aspect, such as Automation engineering space in manufacturing process to achieve digital manufacturing benefits to any businesses in the future. Such as reducing cost, shortening manufacturing time, raising efficiency, shortening delivery products to client individual time. How can artificial intelligence give the need and advanced fast and evaluation methods benefits for space exploration? When US NASA (space exploration organization) achieves any space exploration missions, it will answer this question:
When is it useful to have a machine use (AI) technology to achieve a decision? After all, after millions of years of space exploration and rough 10,000 years of civilization, humans are usually quite good at making decisions in complex uncertain environments. Through, Johns Hoplains University's Applied Physical Lab. Research in (AI) technology enabled systems, which has identified three general use cases for (AI) technology to

explore space mission:

First, for some tasks (AI) technology is more cost effectiveness than human. Second, (AI) technology is better suited than humans at solving some, but not all problems. Third, (AI) technology allows NASA organization's space exploration mission to develop machines that ate capable of responding faster than when a human is in the decision loop (D. Scheidt, 2012, A. Castano et. al. 2008).

So, the use of (AI) technology to enable science by observing the pace of rapidly evolving phenomena was demonstrated. It is more effectively coordinating and (AI) technology utilizing to earn economic benefits to use for space exploration mission.

However, (AI) technology also have current risk for space exploration. Today (AI) technology is immature and requires further development to reach its potential. For instance, the (AI) technology algorithms that detected the dust derive could not have identified whether the Martain weather represented a threat to the cover. Also it can not yet use instrument input to determine what, where and how to autonomously make the next space science measurement. An equally important factor limiting (AI)'s deployment is that lacks the methodology and technology to effectively test (AI) technology. So, the challenge will testing (AI) enabled system is how (AI) performance can be measured. It would be NASA organization's difficulty to find (AI) technology to develop to carry on researching any space exploration missions in the future. However, (AI) technology will be a good economic benefit choice for space exploration mission in the future.

● What is artificial intelligence potential
benefits and ethical considerations?

The ability of (AI) technology systems to transform vast amounts of complex information into insight has the potential to help solve manufacturing or service challenges for human needs. However, to reap the societal benefits of (AI) systems, humans will need to trust then and make sure that which follow the same ethical principles, moral values, professional codes and social norms that we humans would follow in the same scenario, research and educational efforts as well as carefully designed regulation in order to achieve the most effort of economic benefits goals. For example, international business machines corporation (IBM) is actively engaged both competitors , in global discussions about how to make (AI) ethical and as beneficial as possible for people as social economic benefits. (AI) is usually defined as the " capability of a computer program to perform tasks or reasoning processes " that human usually associate to intelligence in a human being. Often, it has to do with the ability to make a good decision, even when there is uncertainty, too much information to handle. As an example, play chess or complex card games of entertainment activities is believed to need some form of intelligence in a human being, as well as choosing the best medical facilities in a difficult medical case, or creating something new, such as mathematical theorem or even some form of act, or even driving automatic machine man (self driving vehicle) replacing human driving in the middle of a crowded city.

(AI) needs depends on what we consider being intelligence in the behavior of a human being act a certain point in time. If human belief about human intelligence changes and we don't believe any longer that a certain task requires intelligence, then a computer program performing that task is no longer part of (AI), it becomes just another boring computer program. So, it means that (AI) technology will replace some old computer programs, if human can invent new generation of (AI) software for any functions or activities to satisfy human needs.

As IBM, it argues intelligence. This means that we aim to build systems that enhance and scale human expertise and skills rather than replacing them. We therefore focus on practical applications of (AI) capabilities that assist people in performing well-defined tasks of needs by exploiting and wide range of (AI)-based services. We also use the term " cognitive computing" it is mean a comprehensive net of capabilities based on technology. It comprises the fields of machine learning, reasoning and decision technologies, language, speech and vision recognition and processing technologies, high performance and high efficient functions for any industries or individual consumers needs. For example, robotics, which are usually very good at doing what which are supposed to in any environment, much have public shopping center, factory etc. places which need simply services from the robot (machine man), such as cleans the floor of our houses to the robot that can work together with humans in production chains, passing through the warehouse, robots can take care of the tasks of an entire warehouse and the companion robots like Nao, Pepper, Aibo and Giraff, who can entertain use, talk to use and help elderly people to stay connected to their friends, relatives and doctors.

Google company is building automatic machine (self-driving cars) and has acquired more than 10 robotics companies. Facebook had opened whole new research facility only on (AI) research. Apply computer has developed

Siri. Microsoft computer company has built a similar personalized assistant. Google has Deep mind, a UK company whose long term aim is to build general (AI) and has already great potential to win game to the world champion and IBM is investing a huge amount of resources in applying its Watson cognitive computing system to the medical domains to finance and to personalized education. In Europe, IBM is establishing new centers in Munich and Milan focused in the application of cognitive computer capabilities to the internet of things and healthcare respectively.

For example, automatic machine man (self-driving cars) are all about (AI), which used to be able to see what happens in the street (signals ,lanes, other cars, pedestrians, traffic lights, which need to able predict what other cars and pedestrians will do, and who need to be able to cope with unforeseen situations. Since, most car accidents are due to human fault, it is estimated that the adoption of self-driving cars will save about half of the lives that are usually last in car accidents.

IBM Watson company has to understand spoken language, make sense of massive amount to text , respond correctly to questions in many categories, as well as assess its own confidence in responding to such questions. In the future, (AI) technology can own question/answering capabilities that would be very useful, for example, in assisting a doctor when trying to some to the correct diagnosis for a patient and to propose the best therapy .

Intelligent machines can also rely on huge amounts of data to be used to learn how to make better decisions. This data comes from all of us over the years Facebook users have uploaded more than 250 billion pictures and every day who upload about 350 million more. Every second, we submit 40,000 google search queries. So, (AI) technology will be connected through the web from appliances to traffic lights from cars to watches. Other tasks that are very easy for humans are physical and manipulation tasks, such as walking , running, picking up an object to make its shape and location, restricted environment. But (AI) machine man technology still not able to have the general physical and manipulation capabilities even of a 6 year old.

So, it brings this question: Why do (AI) scientists need to concern ethics? Because (AI) technology is complex, information into insight has the potential to reveal long held secrets and help solve some of the world's most difficult problems. (AI) systems can potentially be used to help discover insights to treat disease, predict the whether, and manage the global economy. So, ethic issues is important to and (AI) scientists . If any one new

(AI) technology research investigation could success, it will be a secret to and the (AI) scientists can not permit to their loyalty to any competitors to damage the fair (AI) technology products trading market. The country (countries) (AI) technology scientists need to concern ethic issues, who need to keep secrets for their countries economic or/and social benefits. This is moral issues to any countries/country loyalty is whose countries intangible assets. They can not sell (AI) loyalty to any their countries to assist whose economic benefits immorally.

● How can (AI) technology influence to global health care economy development?

According to (AI) lecturer analysis, when combined key clinical health (AI) application can potentially create $150 billion in annual savings for the US healthcare economy by 2026 year. (AI) technology is re-winning modern conception of healthcare delivery. It enables machines to sense, comprehend, act and learn. So which can perform administrative and clinical healthcare functions (Accenture, 2017).

It will help health care service organizations to reduce health care cost, will improve and raise service quality and access. So, (AI) health market size will be predicted growth. (AI) applications in health care include robot-assisted surgery, virtual nursing assistant, administrative workflow assistant, fraud detection, error reduction connected machines, clinical trial participant identifier, preliminary diagnosis, automated image diagnosis and cybersecurity.

What kind of benefits (AI) technology can contribute to healthcare service? (AI) technology can deliver what many health care organizations need, such as financial and operational of labor costs, digital expectations from patient consumers how to use (AI) technology to solve interoperability challenges in any healthcare organizations. Also (AI) technology can be applied to wellness an d lifestyle management, diagnostics, delivers financially but also way of organizational and workflow improvement. So, (AI) technology will be continue to become most prevalent and adoption to healthcare organizations , which must need to enhance structure to be position to take full advantages of new (AI) technological capabilities. (AI) technology can change the nature of work and employment is rapidly changing to make the best use of both humans and (AI) talent in healthcare industry in the future. For example, (AI) technology offers a way to fill in gaps and the rising labor shortage in healthcare. According to Accenture analysis, the physicians shortage is increasing. However, (AI) technology will manufacture healthcare machine men to replace physicians in future one day(2017). Hence, (AI) technology will be invented to raise health care service staffs work efficiency and performance in any hospitals or clinics in the future.

In conclusion, (AI) technology will raise efficiency for any service or manufacturing industries in the future, although, it is possible that it will also rise low skillful workers unemployment numbers. But, the most important influence to human technological innovation will be risen and it will influence human life will be changed to be better, e.g. self drive cars, health care physician machine men, machine man cleaners etc. intelligent machine men will be manufactured to serve for our daily life. Furthermore, (AI) technological products will influence countries trading, some low technological development countries manufacturing businessmen can choose to buy any (AI) products to raise whose productivity and efficiency and reducing cost to achieve economic cost saving result. Also, GDP of trading growth income will increase to the (AI) products sale countries. Hence, it will be beneficial to economic development to both developed and developing countries both in the future as well as (AI) scientists time and money spending will be valued to continue to invest (AI) technology development for human life and economy benefits for long term.

In conclusion (AI) technology will raise macro economy growth and it can create many (AI) jobs , but it also raise the low level technological worker unemployment change. In the future, (AI) technology can be applied to digital technology to attempt to invent any new undiscovered (AI) and digital technology. So, it needs any scientists to continue to research how digital and (AI) technology can be mixed to satisfy human's future undiscovered needs.

CHAPTER SEVEN

Artificial intelligence education development or the future of defense choice

Nowadays, artificial intelligence (AI) is widely knowledge to be one kind of the dramatic technology. However, it is expected to continue, to have a disruptive impact on human's private and public life, so defense and security will be no exception. But how exactly will these be affected ? How will (AI) defense and security is incremental in nature?

To research why artificial intelligence (AI) has possible to be used to cause autonomous weapons by human. We need to understand these three aspects of relationship. They include cybersecurity and artificial intelligence and machine learning and autonomous weapon systems relationship between of them.

Firstly, we need to know what is the mean of artificial intelligence and cyber defense/offense? It means defense of critical networks: real time, pattern finding, anomaly seeking, it must utilize machine (AI) learning algorithms to efficiently, and instantaneously respond to potential network threats as well as it means human on or out of the loop. On the loop : it means anomaly detection: human notified, IT analysis, response. Out of the loop: it means anomaly detection: (AI) decides best method of response: quarantine, honey pot monitoring, hack-back. Thus, it is possible that (AI) can be used , such as autonomous cyber weapon.

What is artificial intelligence and autonomous weapons? Autonomous weapons mean one kind of weapon that can be selected and engaged a target, without intervention by a human operator. Are these machines artificially intelligent? I believe the answer is not, because present weapons systems are not capable of human level reasoning. But, (AI) algorithms are presently employed to process sensor data, monitor system health, take and respond to vocal commands manage data, navigate. This, future autonomous weapons systems will require stronger (AI) to be secure and operationally and cost effective. Moreover, self-aware autonomous cyber systems are crucial.

What is cybersecurity mean? It means the ability to control access to networked systems and the information they contain. It is acted to prevent , detect, recover, react. It is application objects concern people, process, technology and it's application goals are confidentiality, integrity and popular availability. Thus, what is cyber weapon mean? Walware means viruses, Trojans, zero-days, worms ransomware, spyware etc. Does it require a particular objective? E.g. military paramilitary or intelligence. Does it require physical harm? E.g. functional harm or interruption? Mental harm? Is (AI) a technological weapon that it is an object or tool? What about when it is an weapon agent?

In simplicity, (AI) can be one of scientific weapons platform. When one day, it is invented to be applied to control war planes to fly to any countries to attack enemies or it is invented to be seemed to human to replace soldiers to bring guns or any weapons go to other countries to attack. So, it is possible that future any war defense planes, (AI) technological automatic control weapon can be replaced of human soldiers or war plane pilots to control any war defense planes to go to different enemy countries to attack them easily. It is very horror matter to threaten global human's ourselves life in the future , if (AI) automatic control war defense planes or (AI) automatic control machine soldiers were invented successfully.

Hence , when (AI) can be applied to weapons platforms, it structures that launch weapons, i.e. jets, ships, vehicles. (AI) platform and weapon and software architecture components are be done one (AI) technological weapons learning systems. Thus, human will encounter any (AI) benefits or risks (threats) causes in the same time as soon as possible. If we can predict when (AI) weapon system will be manufactured or invented successfully. Then, we can reduce (AI) weapon systems risks , if we can threaten any (AI) scientists continue to invent any undiscovered (AI) weapons in any time to avoid the future first time (AI) weapon war occurrence in possible.

The (AI) weapon system risk means autonomy: the ability to problem solve technological war , when (AI) weapon system is manufactured successfully, the power to act, how to damage the (AI) weapon system.

The power to chance to stop (AI) weapon system manufacturing processes, ability to create a new goals, how to change the (AI) weapon system inventors' or scientists' minds to avoid to apply (AI) tools to achieve attack goals to change to another positive goal. Due to human can't know a prior what an autonomous (AI) weapon system will do.

Although, human is known what (AI) is , but human is also known when (AI) scientists whose emergent behaviors will do to change to do any negative behaviors from positive behaviors. Whatever (AI) weapon system design we use, there will be cybersecurity, problems arising from computation design/complexity. Due to any one (AI) scientist can manipulate the system to act against itself, or who can utilize traditional " cyber weapons" against the (AI) weapon system, or who can manipulate the system to lie to humans, but also due to complexity, there is no way to know if it is lying or not or bounded rationality : satisficing.

Finally, the most serious (AI) technological invention risks are human is unknown these aspects of (AI) absolutely: They are not simple automatic systems, learning reasoning, communication of " self-aware" systems. Thus, human will face (AI) technological invention risks or threats. We need to find any methods to avoid (AI) weapon system is manufactured successfully to avoid (AI) technological war can occur in future anyone day. Consequently, why (AI) scientists do not choose to invent (AI) machine men own human reading, writing, speaking, judgement, analyizing abilities to develop human's future education industry, but they choose to invent (AI) machine men own human weapon to attack enemy ability.
Hence, (AI) scientists have moral responsibilities to avoid to invent (AI) machine men to own human's attack abilities. I shall indicate future what aspects of (AI) machine men can be applied to different education industry aspects as below:

7.1 Online technology and online book
technology influences artificial intelligence
mind development

Nowadays, online technological invention bring online book technological development. Also, artificial intelligent technological machine men had been invented to link internet to do any jobs, e.g. children can find any data from artificial intelligent machine men when the artificial intelligent machine man had been installed internet and computer function, then children can find any online books to read from the artificial intelligent machine man. Such as Japan artificial intellgent machine men had installed computer and internet function, the Japan family children can find any online books to read from the artificial intelligent machine man at Japan any families' homes conveniently. Hence, it implies that future one day, artificial intelligent machine has possible to be invented to own human's reading and/or writing abilities.

For example,online book publishing is one kind of popular internet technology. For example, Amazon publish is as a business model with many potential advantages, relative to a physical operation. It held out the potential of lower book inventing and distribution costs and reduced overhead. Consumers could find the books, they were looking for more easily and a variety book topic choices could be offered for sale. It can accept and fulfill orders from almost any domestic location with equal ease. And most purchasers made on its site would be exempt from sales tax. One Amazon strategy hand, it would have to make its returns and redress processes transparent and reliable, and offer other ways for clients to learn, as much about the book possible before buying. Future online book market development trend, such as Amazon, Barnes & Noble etc. online book shops.

Hence, online book store technology can be applied to artificial intelligent technology. Such as artificial intelligent machine men can apply computer technology to learn the abilities of reading and/or writing any books either on paper or on computer. Hence, it is possible that artificial intelligent machine men will have similar human's writing and/or reading books ability when they own human's mind ability. However, it bring this questions: Can artificial intelligent machine men own human's mind abilities? If they own human's mind abilities, is it mean that they can write and/or read any books? Can artificial intelligent machine men own human's mind abilities to create to write any books? Can artificial intelligent machine men own human's mind abilities to read and make any judgements or decisions more accurate than human's judgements or decisions? To answer these questions? I shall indicate that online book reading and writing technology can be applied to artificial intelligent machine men reading and writing technology. Because they are similiar computer mind technological development. So, I believe that future artificial intelligence machine men can be invented to own similar human's reading and writing's mind abilities in future one day.

I believe artificial intelligence and online technological reading abilities are very similiar. Nowadays, computer can be invented to attempt to read and write any books by human. Why can not artificial intelligent machine men replace computer to read and write any books? Artificial intelligent machine men can replace human to attempt to write or/and read books, due to artificial intelligent machine men had invented to own human mind to do some jobs and their mind had been invented to be similiar to human behavioral abilities to do these behaviors, e.g. cooking, driving, playing games, singing songs, speaking, listening, frighting etc. different human's abilities. So, it seems that artificial intelligent will be possible to be invented to own human's mind abilities to do any writing or reading behaviors or functions.

7.2 Prediction of artificial intelligence

reading and writing abilities

development

What is future trend of artificial intelligence reading and writing abilities development? To answer this question, we need to know what benefits of artificial intelligent machine men can attribute to human's needs when they can own any human's mind to read or/and write any books.

I shall indicate e-books reading and writing example, if artificial intelligent machine men can be invented to own human's mind to write and/or read e-books on computer. Then, it brings this question: Can artificial intelligent machine men assist human to learn to do judgement to solve any challenges?

I believe that when artificial intelligent machine men can be invented to own human mind to write or/and read any books, then they will own human's mind ability to make judgement to solve any challenges more accurately, even their decisions can be more accurate to compare to human's decisions. So, artificial intelligent machine mens' writing and reading ability is the main factor to cause their mind to do any judgement in order to make any decisions more accurately. Consequently, in future one day, artificial intelligent machine mens' writing and reading ability will be invented to similar human's reading and writing abilities as well as their minds can also be invented to similar human's minds as well as their judgement abilities can be invented to similar to human's judgement abilities to make any decisions more accurate.

7.3 The influences when AI is invented to own human's mind and judgement abilities

Finally, I shall discuss what are the influences when AI is invented to own human's mind and judgement abilities in our future job market. The achievement of artificial intelligent (AI) machine men achievement requirement of owning human's mind and judgement abilities which requires extensive manual labor, and by augmenting the calling process with machine learning, the process where speed and accuracy are needed to close to human's mind and judgement abilities. Expert human race callers now have better information at artificial intelligent machine men at their fingertips faster.

Hence, if the above those requirements are achieved to satisfy artificial intelligent machine men ind and judgement abilities demand to close or exceed humans' mind and judgement abilities. Then, I believe that future human's some simple jobs must be replaced by (AI) machine men. Even, human's some professonal jobs, e.g. lawyer, accountant, administator, typing etc. professional skillful jobs, which will be either replaced or will be assisted by (AI) machine men. For example, (AI) machine men learn how to type english or other language words to do typing job ; they can learn how to apply accounting knowledge to record any firm's income and expenditure record of accounting job; they can also learn how to assist architects to design any architectural building drawing plans to do architect jobs; they can learn how to analyze any court evidences to judge any criminal or civil cases and assist lawyers to give legal advices to achieve more reasonable judgement for any legal cases; they can also learn how to assist firm's managers or administrators to manage any organization teams efficiently.

Consequently, when (AI) machine men can be invented to achieve to exceed human's mind and judgement abilities level. Then, I believe that they can do instead of human' simple jobs, which can do even human's more difficult and more judgement requirement of professional skillful jobs. So, (AI) machine men must need to achieve to do any jobs, they are same, even exceed to human professionals' abilities. Then, it will cause a lot of human's jobs to be disappeared or some human's jobs will be replaced by owning judgement and mind abilities of (AI) machine men to do.

Hence, future many human's jobs will be replaced by technological labors. Employers choose to buy (AI) machine men to replace human labors. The reasons include (AI) machine men have none unhappy, angry emotin to influence their low efficiencies and low productivities. Their judgement and mind abilities can exceed human's abilities or do any jobs to compare better performance to human's abilities. Consequently, different occupation labors need to prepare to learn how to co-operate with (AI) machine men to let future employers feel (AI) machine men will be human's assistant to assist human to do jobs efficiently when human and (AI) machine men work together. It aims to avoid future employers feel (AI) machine men's judgement and mind abilities can exceed any low knowledgeable and skilful occupation labors, even high knowledge and skilful occupation labors. It means that (AI) machine men are only labors' assistant if (AI) machine mens' judgement and mind abilities are below under to human labors' judgement and mind abilities.

Consequently, to avoid (AI) machine men can replace human to do any simple or complex jobs to cause any future any occupation labors' competitiors. I recommend that it is right time labors ought prepare to learn different skills. So, every individual labor does not only concentrate on one kind of skill. Because supposing one kind of the occupation labor's job duties are replaced by (AI) machine men. If the employee had owned more than one kind of occupation skill. Then, I believe that who can avoid the unemployment threat more easier than the employee only owned one kind of occupation skill, when (AI) machine men had invented to own human's mind and judgement abilities in future one day. The most important, I believe that (AI) invention will be applied to be teach how to learn human's skills and mind ability. Such as education industy, teacher won't be replaced by (AI), otherwise, (AI) will be teacher's assistant to help them to do education data gather or teaching jobs. So, teachers won't be replaced by (AI), otherwise, teachers will depend on (AI) data gather or teaching job to give them opinions how to solve student's teaching challenges as well as teachers can concentrate on researching education jobs for schools' benefits if (AI) technology can be invented to on human's mind and judgement and reading and writing abilities in the future.

7.4
Artificial intelligence and the future of defense
or teaching choice

Nowadays, artificial intelligence (AI) is widely knowledge to be one kind of the dramatic technology. However, it is expected to continue, to have a disruptive impact on human's private and public life, so defense and security will be no exception. But how exactly will these be affected ? How will (AI) defense and security is incremental in nature? If (AI) technological machine men are applied to teach students in education aspect, is it better to my next generation learning develpment more than they are applied to war attack aspect.

To research why artificial intelligence (AI) has possible to be used to cause autonomous weapons by human. We need to understand these three aspects of relationship. They include cybersecurity and artificial intelligence and machine learning and autonomous weapon systems relationship between of them. Basic on (AI) machine can be invented to learn any new knowledge, so if (AI) machine men are taught how to attack enemy, which will be such as human soldier function. But, if (AI) machine men are taught how to learn university knowledge to teach students. Then, they will be such as human lecturer function. So, when (AI) is invented to own human mind and judgement and learning abilities, then they will be either human's enemy or human's assistant, such as university lecturer's assistant.

Firstly, we need to know what is the mean of artificial intelligence and cyber defense/offense? It means defense of critical networks: real time, pattern finding, anomaly seeking, it must utilize machine (AI) learning algorithms to efficiently, and instantaneously respond to potential network threats as well as it means human on or out of the loop. On the loop : it means anomaly detection: human notified, IT analysis, response. Out of the loop: it means anomaly detection: (AI) decides best method of response: quarantine, honey pot monitoring, hack-back. Thus, it is possible that (AI) can be used , such as autonomous cyber weapon. If (AI) is applied to make the decision best method of response to learning aspect, such as univeristy different subject knowledge. Then, it will be one good technological educational tool to teach university students.

In simplicity, (AI) can be one of scientific weapons platform or one of university teaching tool. When one day, it is invented to be applied to control war planes to fly to any countries to attack enemies or it is invented to be seemed to human to replace soldiers to bring guns or any weapons go to other countries to attack. So, it is possible that future any war defense planes, (AI) technological automatic control weapon can be replaced of human soldiers or war plane pilots to control any war defense planes to go to different enemy countries to attack them easily. It is very horror matter to threaten global human's ourselves life in the future , if (AI) automatic control war defense planes or (AI) automatic control machine soldiers were invented successfully. Otherwise, when one day, (AI) machine lecturer is invented to be applied to learn university different subjects knowledge to replace lecturers to copy lecturer's every prepared lecturer course to speak to let students to listen when they are sitting in university halls as well as the (AI) machine lecturer can make analysis and judgement response to answer every student's enquire immediately after it had speaking all courses to students to listen in lecturer hall every time. Then, it can let human lecturer does any education job duty, e.g. research education work. So, (AI) machine lecturer will be future human lecturer's assistant in future one day.

Finally, the most serious (AI) technological invention risks are human is unknown these aspects of (AI) absolutely: They are not simple automatic systems, learning reasoning, communication of " self-aware" systems. Thus, human will face (AI) technological invention risks or threats if human invent (AI) machine man to learn how to attack enemy. Otherwise, if human invent (AI) machine man to learn how to teach univerity student. I believe that my future university students can raise learn ability and writing ability and reading ability from (AI) machine lecturer teaching more than human lecturer teaching.

7.5
Online technology and online book
technology influences artificial intelligence
mind development

Nowadays, online technological invention bring online book technological development. Also, artificial intelligent technological machine men had been invented to link internet to do any jobs, e.g. children can find any data from artificial intelligent machine men when the artificial intelligent machine man had been installed internet and computer function, then children can find any online books to read from the artificial intelligent machine man. Such as Japan artificial intellgent machine men had installed computer and internet function, the Japan family children can find any online books to read from the artificial intelligent machine man at Japan any families' homes conveniently. Hence, it implies that future one day, artificial intelligent machine has possible to be invented to own human's reading and/or writing abilities.

For example,online book publishing is one kind of popular internet technology. For example, Amazon publish is as a business model with many potential advantages, relative to a physical operation. It held out the potential of lower book inventing and distribution costs and reduced overhead. Consumers could find the books, they were looking for more easily and a variety book topic choices could be offered for sale. It can accept and fulfill orders from almost any domestic location with equal ease. And most purchasers made on its site would be exempt from sales tax. One Amazon strategy hand, it would have to make its returns and redress processes transparent and reliable, and offer other ways for clients to learn, as much about the book possible before buying. Future online book market development trend, such as Amazon, Barnes & Noble etc. online book shops.

Hence, online book store technology can be applied to artificial intelligent technology. Such as artificial intelligent machine men can apply computer technology to learn the abilities of reading and/or writing any books either on paper or on computer. Hence, it is possible that artificial intelligent machine men will have similar human's writing and/or reading books ability when they own human's mind ability. However, it bring this questions: Can artificial intelligent machine men own human's mind abilities? If they own human's mind abilities, is it mean that they can write and/or read any books? Can artificial intelligent machine men own human's mind abilities to create to write any books? Can artificial intelligent machine men own human's mind abilities to read and make any judgements or decisions more accurate than human's judgements or decisions? To answer these questions? I shall indicate that online book reading and writing technology can be applied to artificial intelligent machine men reading and writing technology. Because they are similiar computer mind technological development. So, I believe that future artificial intelligence machine men can be invented to own similar human's reading and writing's mind abilities in future one day.

I believe artificial intelligence and online technological reading abilities are very similiar. Nowadays, computer can be invented to attempt to read and write any books by human. Why can not artificial intelligent machine men replace computer to read and write any books? Artificial intelligent machine men can replace human to attempt to write or/and read books, due to artificial intelligent machine men had invented to own human mind to do some jobs and their mind had been invented to be similiar to human behavioral abilities to do these behaviors, e.g. cooking, driving, playing games, singing songs, speaking, listening, frighting etc. different human's abilities. So, it seems that artificial intelligent will be possible to be invented to own human's mind abilities to do any writing or reading behaviors or functions.

7.6 Prediction of artificial intelligence
     reading and writing abilities

development

What is future trend of artificial intelligence reading and writing abilities development? To answer this question, we need to know what benefits of artificial intelligent machine men can attribute to human's needs when they can own any human's mind to read or/and write any books.

I shall indicate e-books reading and writing example, if artificial intelligent machine men can be invented to own human's mind to write and/or read e-books on computer. Then, it brings this question: Can artificial intelligent machine men assist human to learn to do judgement to solve any challenges?

I believe that when artificial intelligent machine men can be invented to own human mind to write or/and read any books, then they will own human's mind ability to make judgement to solve any challenges more accurately, even their decisions can be more accurate to compare to human's decisions. So, artificial intelligent machine mens' writing and reading ability is the main factor to cause their mind to do any judgement in order to make any decisions more accurately. Consequently, in future one day, artificial intelligent machine mens' writing and reading ability will be invented to similar human's reading and writing abilities as well as their minds can also be invented to similar human's minds as well as their judgement abilities can be invented to similar to human's judgement abilities to make any decisions more accurate.

7.7 The influences when AI is invented to own
human's mind and judgement abilities

Finally, I shall discuss what are the influences when AI is invented to own human's mind and judgement abilities in our future job market. The achievement of artificial intelligent (AI) machine men achievement requirement of owning human's mind and judgement abilities which requires extensive manual labor, and by augmenting the calling process with machine learning, the process where speed and accuracy are needed to close to human's mind and judgement abilities. Expert human race callers now have better information at artificial intelligent machine men at their fingertips faster.

Hence, if the above those requirements are achieved to satisfy artificial intelligent machine men ind and judgement abilities demand to close or exceed humans' mind and judgement abilities. Then, I believe that future human's some simple jobs must be replaced by (AI) machine men. Even, human's some professonal jobs, e.g. lawyer, accountant, administator, typing etc. professional skillful jobs, which will be either replaced or will be assisted by (AI) machine men. For example, (AI) machine men learn how to type english or other language words to do typing job ; they can learn how to apply accounting knowledge to record any firm's income and expenditure record of accounting job; they can also learn how to assist architects to design any architectural building drawing plans to do architect jobs; they can learn how to analyze any court evidences to judge any criminal or civil cases and assist lawyers to give legal advices to achieve more reasonable judgement for any legal cases; they can also learn how to assist firm's managers or administrators to manage any organization teams efficiently.

Consequently, when (AI) machine men can be invented to achieve to exceed human's mind and judgement abilities level. Then, I believe that they can do instead of human' simple jobs, which can do even human's more difficult and more judgement requirement of professional skillful jobs. So, (AI) machine men must need to achieve to do any jobs, they are same, even exceed to human professionals' abilities. Then, it will cause a lot of human's jobs to be disappeared or some human's jobs will be replaced by owning judgement and mind abilities of (AI) machine men to do.

Hence, future many human's jobs will be replaced by technological labors. Employers choose to buy (AI) machine men to replace human labors. The reasons include (AI) machine men have none unhappy, angry emotin to influence their low efficiencies and low productivities. Their judgement and mind abilities can exceed human's abilities or do any jobs to compare better performance to human's abilities. Consequently, different occupation labors need to prepare to learn how to co-operate with (AI) machine men to let future employers feel (AI) machine men will be human's assistant to assist human to do jobs efficiently when human and (AI) machine men work together. It aims to avoid future employers feel (AI) machine men's judgement and mind abilities can exceed any low knowledgeable and skilful occupation labors, even high knowledge and skilful occupation labors. It means that (AI) machine men are only labors' assistant if (AI) machine mens' judgement and mind abilities are below under to human labors' judgement and mind abilities.

Consequently, to avoid (AI) machine men can replace human to do any simple or complex jobs to cause any future any occupation labors' competitiors. I recommend that it is right time labors ought prepare to learn different skills. So, every individual labor does not only concentrate on one kind of skill. Because supposing one kind of the occupation labor's job duties are replaced by (AI) machine men. If the employee had owned more than one kind of occupation skill. Then, I believe that who can avoid the unemployment threat more easier than the employee only owned one kind of occupation skill, when (AI) machine men had invented to own human's mind and judgement abilities in future one day.

7.8
Why does AI machine lecturer can raise
education quality?

When (AI) machine men can own human reading and writing and judgement and analytical abilities, then they can replace university lecturers to teach students to raise students' learning abilities absolutely. Then, it bring this question: Why does I machine lecturer can raise education quality? Why do universities prefer to apply (AI) machine lecturer to teach teachers more than human lectuer in university lecturer hall learning environment? Will (AI) university lecturers replace human lecturers to teach students to learn at university lecturing halls popularly? Can (AI) university lecturers replace university human lecturers to teach students more easily and it can let students feel more easily to learn when they are listening what (AI) university lecturers are teaching to them every time university lecture.

In university today, nearly all students need to attend university lecturing hall to listen their lecturer's teaching in every time course. However, many students do not feel interesting to attend university halls to listen human lecturer's teaching. The reasons include, they are busy, so no time to attend lecturer's hall to listen lecturer's teaching; or they feel bore to listen their lecturer's teaching; they feel difficulty to learn; they have confidence to exam and do their assignments, so they feel that they do not need to go to lecturing halls to listen their human lecturer's teaching. However, if one day, (AI) machine lecturers are invented to teach university students to learn and solve their learning difficulties. Can it raise student individual learning interest, due to (AI) machine lecturers' education quality is better than human lecturers' education quality?

What will influence to university students if (AI) machine lecturer can invented to replace human lecture? The influences will include such as below:

First reason: the only way is going to be useful to university lecturers are if all (AI) machine lecturers are well-informed and fully supported to assist human lectuers to teach whose students to let them to listen whose teaching absolutely. So, human lecturers can concentrate on doing any education research and data gathering jobs to prepare for (AI) machine lecturers to help them to explain human lecturers' every time prepared course contents more efficiently. So, (AI) machine lectuers can help human lecturers to share whose teaching time in lecturing halls. Human lecturers' can spend whose hall lecturing time to do whose educational research or other educational gathering jobs absolutely.

The second reason, the human lecturer (Human capital) has ability and efficiency of concentrating on education data gatehering research jobs to prepare to write whose books. When (AI) machine lecturer replace the human lecturer to spend time to attend lecturing hall to teach students. Fo long term, the human lecturer can raise education productivity growth and education quality raising, due to who only concentrate on searching or gathering data to prepare to write whose books to raise their education level.

In macro and micro economic view, the well (AI) machine lecturer educated labor (human capital) is often replaced to human lecturer as one of the critical factors to influence rapid education productivities and educational quality growth to the Asia developing countries' any regions or cities. Because any of these Asia developing countries, such as China,

Korea, Philippines etc. countries which need have well educated and knowledgeable lecturer labors to raise any universities' educational productivities and educational qualities growth. So (AI) assistant lecturer factors which ought have close relationship to cause the good or bad future student learning effectiveness and education or learning qualities raising in these any one of Asia developing countries.

The third reason, for the big population of student growth number example, China's student growth rate is larger than school growth rate. If China expect every students have enough chance to study in schools, but university human lectuer numbers are not enough to supply to universities to teach their students. I believe that (AI) machine lecturer is only one kind of teaching method to solve these big population countries' university lectuer number shortage challenge.

In conclusion, in long term, (AI) machine lecturers can solve university human lecturer shortage challenge as well as they can attract many students to attend lecturing halls and human lecturers can raise education quality when they can concentrate on searching or gathering data to prepare their education career, when (AI) machine lectuers replace them to spend time to attend univesity halls to teach students in every university lecturing time.

7.9

Future AI machine education market

I believe that when AI (artificial intelligent machine men) which can invented to own to similar to human mind, learning, language, analytical, judgement abilites. Then, which can be applied to any education market service industy. (AI) potential education market service industy includes such as below:

● (AI) university lecture assistant

Future (AI) machine men can assist univerity lectuers to attend university halls to attempt to teach university students for different subjects, e.g. english, math, economic, math, engineering, art, architect etc. different subjects. It depends on the human lectuter who prepares to spend time to teach the (AI) machine lecturer to remember whose teaching subject. For example, the economic lecturer spend one year time to teach the (AI) machine lecturer to learn all economic knowledge. Then, the (AI) machine lecturer can use its machine brain to remember all the human lecturer's economic concepts and prepared teaching economic contents within the one year. Hence, after one year the (AI) machine lecturer can remember all the human lecturer's economic concepts and economic theories and economic contents to prepare to attend university lecturing halls to teach all first year undergraduated first year economic students confidently. It means that the human lecturer's job duties will change to teach (AI) machine lecturer to learn whose economic knowledge to prepare to let the (AI) machine lecturer to replace whom to teach whose university students; so the human lectuer can spend more time to do other research job for whose university education development. Hence, the (AI) machine lecturer can share the human lecturer teaching job as well as the human lectuer can concentrate on spending time to do whose research jobs for whose university education development. This is one both win strategy to university and the lecturer if (AI) machine lecturer is invented to assist future university lecturer's teaching jobs.

● (AI) secondary and primary teacher assistant

In the future (AI) technolgical development, instead of (AI) machine men can be applied to university education aspect. Future (AI) machine men can also be applied to secondary and primary teaching aspect. For example, primary and secondary schools do not need attend classroom to teach students. (AI) machine teachers can replace them to attempt to do teaching job. They only need to spend one year time to prepare to teach (AI) machine teacher to learn how to apply their teaching skill concern their subjects who need to teach to their students, e.g. english language writing and reading and spelling skill, sing song skill, drawing picture skill, calculation skill etc. different studying skill. Then, the (AI) primary or secondary machine teacher can apply the primary or sendary human teacher skills to attempt yo teach whose students. Hence, the primary and secondary human teacher whose duties will change to learn how to teach whose teaching skills to let the (AI) primary or seondary machine lecturer to remember how to apply human skills to teach whose students for different subjects, such as, english writing and reading and spelling language skills, singing songs language skills, math calculation skills etc. Hence, future primary or secondary school teachers who responsibilities will change to learn how to teach (AI) machine teacher teaching skills to prepare to replace them to teach their students in classroom.

● (AI) scientific research assistant

Future (AI) machine men can be applied to science research aspect, instead of school education job. For example, (AI) machine men can be any scientist's assistant, e.g. space scientist, earth or ocean scientist, human or animal behavioral psychological scientist, climate scientist, chemical scientist, drug scientist etc. How can (AI) machine men can be any kind of scientist to assist scientists to do research jobs ? I shall indiate such as below: For space science example, the (AI) machine space scientist can assist human space scientist to gather space data to assist space scientist to research any undiscovered material to cause our earth, even space. Hence, the space scientist only need to teach the (AI) machine scientist to learn how to help them to apply space technological tools to gather data and then enter all data to computer to record, even the (AI) machine scientist can store all space data discovered record to their machine brain every day. Hence, the human space scientist does not need to spend much time to do gathering data job. The (AI) machine space scientist can help whom to do these space data gathering job, then the human space scientist can concentrate on spendin time to do space research job in whose space science laboratory every day.

For earth science example, the (AI) machine earth scientist can help the earth scientist to go to anywhere to gather earth or ocean natural activity data in our earth every day. Then, the earth scientist only need sit in whose earth laboratory to wait the (AI) machine earth scientist to come to whose laboratory to give whose gathering every day earth or ocean natural activity data to do future research job. Hence, the earth scientist does not need to leave whose laboratory to do any data gathing jobs concern earth or ocean natural activities. The (AI) machine earth or ocean scientist had helped him/her to go to our earth or ocean anywhere to do any earth or ocean activities data gathering jobs every day. Hence, the earth or ocean scientist can concentrate on spending whose time to do any research jobs in laboratory. It means that the (AI) machine earch or ocean scientist had replaced whom to do all outdoor original gathering data jobs.

For these human or animal behavioral psychological scientist, climate scientist, chemical or drug scientist, scientist all examples, the (AI) machine human or animal behavioral psychological scientist can help them to do any data gathering job, e.g. the (AI) machine scientist can learn how to help human or animal behavioral psychological scientist to contact human or animal to observe their daily activities and record all their activities data to transfer all these daily activites data to let the human or animal behavioral psychological scientist to do psychological researching analysis only. The

(AI) machine climate scientist can help the human climate scientist to arrive anywhere to observe climate changes and record climate changes daily. Then, the human climate scientist only need to wait the (AI) machine climate scientist's gathering climate change data record from whose machine brain to do climate changing predict research job in climate laboratory every day. The (AI) chemical or drug machine scientist can help the drug or chemical scientist to gather data of new drug or chemical from internet channel every day. So, the human chemical or drug scientist only need to do researching job after the (AI) machine scientist transfers all daily chemical or drug information to let them to know from internet channel. It means that the chemical or drug human scientist does not need to spend much time to gather drug or chemical new data development trend from internet. The (AI) machine chemical or drug scientist had helped them to do data gathering job every day.

Consequently, future (AI) machine men can do education and research aspects of jobs duties and their role are only human scientists or primary or secondary teachers or university lecturers whose assistants either to share scientist's data gathering job or share teachers or lecturers' teaching job.